Birds and Animals
in Honiton Lace

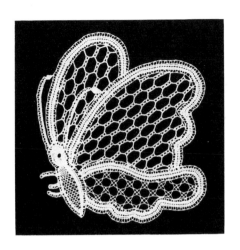

Birds and Animals in Honiton Lace

Saikoh Takano

B.T. Batsford Ltd · London

First published 1992

© Saikoh Takano, 1992

Patterns designed and worked by Saikoh Takano; illustrations and photographs by Yusai Fukuyama. Translations by Marie-Christine Gosse (French), Puck Smelter-Hoekstra (Dutch), and Margarete Wenzel and Brigitte Wichlei (German). The advisor was Lesley Thomas.

Typeset by Lasertext Ltd, Stretford, Manchester, UK

Printed and bound in Great Britain by BPCC Hazells Ltd
Member of BPCC Ltd

Published by
B.T. Batsford Ltd
4 Fitzhardinge Street
London W1H 0AH

A catalogue record for this book is available from the British Library

ISBN 0 7134 6316 3

Contents

Introduction

During my first visit to the UK I was overwhelmed by the very fine lace collections I saw there, especially of Honiton lace, and I visited a great many museums in order to see as much of this beautiful lace as possible.

I found that floral patterns are the most popular in Honiton lace, but both the Royal Albert Memorial Museum and Sidmouth Museum have splendid collections of animal motifs in lace; it was while visiting the Sidmouth collection that I decided I must write a book of animal and bird lace patterns.

This book is primarily intended for those lacemakers with some knowledge of the basic Honiton lace techniques. Photographs show not only the right side of the lace, but also the reverse side, i.e. the working side. These, combined with working diagrams showing the fillings, order of work, and numbers of pairs, give lacemakers all the information they need to re-create these patterns.

I would like to express my sincere appreciation and thanks to my lace teacher, Mrs Elsie Luxton MBE, who introduced me to Honiton lace, and who has willingly given me advice and encouragement ever since. I would also like to thank the museum staff who enabled me to study the lace in their collections.

Saikoh Takano
Tokyo

Einführung

Bei meinem ersten Besuch in England war ich überwältigt von den wunderschönen Spitzensammlungen, die ich dort sah, insbesondere in Honiton Spitze, und ich besuchte eine große Anzahl von Museen, um so viel wie möglich von dieser herrlichen Spitze zu sehen.

Dabei fiel mir auf, daß in der Honiton-Spitze Blumenmuster am häufigsten vertreten sind, doch besitzen sowohl das Royal Albert Memorial Museum als auch das Sidmouth Museum prächtige Sammlungen mit Tiermotiven in Spitze; es war während meines Besuches der Sidmouth-Sammlung, daß ich den Entschluß faßte, ein Spitzen-Buch mit Tier- und Vogelmotiven zu schreiben.

Dieses Buch ist vor allem für die Klöpplerinnen mit einigen Grundkenntnissen in Honiton-Spitze bestimmt.

Die Fotografien zeigen nicht nur die Vorderseite, sondern auch die Rückseite der Spitzen, d.h. die Seite, auf der geklöppelt wird. Zusammen mit den Arbeitszeichnungen, aus denen die Gründe (Füllungen), die Reihenfolge der Ausführung und die Anzahl der Paare ersichtlich sind, bieten sie den Klöpplerinnen alle zum Nacharbeiten nötigen Informationen.

Ich möchte meine aufrichtige Anerkennung und meinen Dank meiner Klöppellehrerin, Frau Elsie Luxton MBE ausdrücken, die mich mit der Honiton-Spitze bekannt machte und mir seitdem mit Rat und Ermunterung zur Seite stand. Ich möchte auch dem Museumspersonal danken, das mir erlaubte, die Spitzen ihrer Sammlungen zu untersuchen.

Saikoh Takano
Tokyo

Inleiding

Tijdens mijn eerste bezoek aan Groot-Brittannië werd ik overweldigd door de schitterende kantverzamelingen die ik daar zag, in het bizonder van Honitonkant. Ik bezocht een groot aantal musea om zoveel mogelijk van deze prachtige kant te zien.

Ik zag dat bloempatronen het populairst zijn in Honiton, maar zowel het Royal Albert Memorial Museum als het Sidmouth Museum hebben een schitterende verzameling diermotieven in kant. Tijdens een bezoek aan het Sidmouth Museum besloot ik een kantboek te schrijven met dier- en vogelpatronen.

Dit boek is in de eerste plaats bedoeld voor kantklosters met enige kennis van de basistechnieken in de Honiton. De foto's tonen niet alleen de goede kant van het werk, maar ook de achterkant, d.i. de werkkant. Ze geven, in combinatie met de werktekeningen van vullingen, werkvolgorde en aantal paren, de kantklosters alle informatie die nodig is om de patronen na te maken.

Ik wil mijn grote waardering en dank uitspreken aan mijn kantlerares Mrs Elsie Luxton MBE, die mij met de Honiton bekend maakte, en die me sindsdien steeds welwillend advies gaf en moed insprak. Ik wil ook de museumstaf bedanken, die me in staat stelde de kant in hun collectie te bestuderen.

Saikoh Takano
Tokyo

Préliminaire

C'est au cours de ma première visite en Angleterre que j'ai découvert avec émerveillement les collections de vieilles dentelles si fines, particulièrement le 'Honiton', et j'ai donc visité beaucoup de musées à la recherche de ces beautés.

Bien que les motifs floraux semblent être très représentatifs du 'Honiton', j'ai remarqué dans les musées Royal Albert Memorial Museum et Sidmouth Museum plusieurs motifs d'animaux en dentelle et c'est pendant la visite du Sidmouth que j'ai décidé de faire un livre de modèles d'animaux et d'oiseaux.

Ce livre s'adresse aux dentellières qui possèdent déjà quelques notions de base du 'Honiton'.

Les photos présentent l'oeuvre finie, mais aussi son envers qui est le côté apparent pour la dentellière en cours de travail. Ainsi, en ajoutant également les diagrammes des fonds, l'ordre de travail, le nombre de paires, les dentellières possèdent toutes les informations nécessaires pour reproduire ces modèles.

Je voudrais adresser mes remerciements et mon admiration à mon professeur Mrs Elsie Luxton MBE qui a guidé mes premiers pas dans la dentelle 'Honiton' et qui m'encourage encore de ses conseils avisés. Je voudrais également remercier l'équipe du musée qui m'a permis ce travail d'après leurs collections.

Saikoh Takano
Tokyo

How to use this book

1 All photographs of the finished work are shown from page 11 to 17 so that comparisons can be easily made and the desired design chosen.

2 Every design is shown in a double-page spread and is illustrated by a photograph of the right side, a photograph of the wrong side, a diagram showing the direction of working, the number of pairs required, and a pricking.

3 Each design has the same numbering for all the illustrations, e.g.

- the right side photograph 1-a,
- the wrong side photograph 1-b,
- the working order 1-c,
- the number of pairs 1-d,
- and the pricking 1-e.

4 The photograph of the wrong side of the lace is shown so that the lacemaker has a direct comparison with his/her work and the author's work during the making of the lace.

5 The patterns have been worked in 180/2 cotton thread (available from Wrigley's of Nottingham) and so the number of threads in the diagrams refers to 180 thread.

When a coarse thread was required DMC Retors d'Alsace no. 50 sewing cotton was used.

6 In the diagram the direction of working is shown by the arrows and the number of pairs of bobbins required for each part is indicated by the number i.e. 5 = 5 pairs or 10 bobbins. 5.5 = 5 pairs and a single thread.

The coarse pair is shown as C, e.g. 6 + C means 6 pairs of bobbins and a coarse pair. 0.5C means a single coarse thread.

The rib is shown as R, e.g. R5 means 5 pairs rib.

7 All prickings in this book are shown in the actual size.

Wie man dieses Buch benutzt

1 Zur Veranschaulichung und leichteren Wahl des zu klöppelnden Motivs sind die Fotos der fertigen Spitzen auf den Seiten 11 bis 17 abgebildet.

2 Jeder Entwurf wird auf einer Doppelseite gezeigt, illustriert durch ein Foto von Vorder und Rückseite der Spitze, einer technischen Zeichnung mit Angabe der erforderlichen Klöppelpaare, des Arbeitsverlaufs sowie des Klöppelbriefes.

3 Zu jedem Entwurf erhalten die dazugehörigen Abbildungen durchweg die gleiche Nummerierung, z.B. Foto Vorderseite der Spitze 1-a, Rückseite 1-b, Arbeitsanleitung 1-c, Anzahl der Klöppelpaare 1-d, Musterbrief 1-e.

4 Im Foto wird die Rückseite (linke Seite) der Spitze gezeigt, damit während des Klöppelns ein direkter Vergleich möglich ist.

5 Die Muster wurden mit Ägyptischen Baumwollgarn 170 geklöppelt, die Anzahl der Fäden im Muster beziehen sich daher stets auf Garnstärke 180. Als Konturfaden wurde Nähgarn DMC Broder Maschine 50 benutzt.

6 In der Arbeitszeichnung wird der Arbeitsverlauf durch Pfeile angegeben, die Anzahl der für die einzelnen Teile erforderlichen Klöppelpaare wird durch entsprechende Zahlen angegeben, z.B. 5 = 5 Paare (10 Klöppel).

Der Konturfaden wird mit 'C' bezeichnet, so bedeutet 6 + C = 6 Klöppelpaare sowie 1 Paar Konturfaden.

Die Rippe wird mit 'R' bezeichnet, R5 bedeutet 5 Paare für die Rippe.

7 Alle Briefe sind in Originalgröße abgebildet.

Hoe dit boek te gebruiken

1 Alle uitgewerkte stukken zijn afgebeeld op blz. 00 tot 00 om het vergelijken en het kiezen van een ontwerp te vergemakkelijken.

2 Elk ontwerp is afgebeeld op een dubbele pagina en wordt toegelicht met foto's van voor- en achterkant, diagrammen voor de werkrichting en het aantal paren, en de prikking.

3 Elk ontwerp heeft voor alle illustraties hetzelfde nummer, bijv.

- de foto van de voorkant 1-a,
- de foto van de achterkant 1-b,
- de werkvolgorde 1-c,
- het aantal paren 1-d,
- en de prikking 1-e.

4 De foto van de achterkant is gegeven opdat de kantwerkster al tijdens het klossen haar werk kan vergelijken met dat van de auteur.

5 De patronen zijn gewerkt in Egyptische Katoen 170, dus de aantallen paren in de diagrammen verwijzen naar garen nr 180. Wanneer een dikke draad nodig was, is naaigaren DMC Broder machine 50 gebruikt.

6 In het diagram is de werkrichting aangegeven door pijlen. Het benodigde aantal paren voor elk deel is aangegeven door nummers, bijv. 5 = 5 paar of 10 klossen.

Het paar met de dikke draad is C, bijv. 6 + C betekent 6 paar plus een paar met dikke draad.

De rib is voorgesteld door R, bijv. R5 betekent rib van 5 paar.

7 Alle prikkingen in het boek zijn op ware grootte gegeven.

Comment utiliser ce livre

1 Toutes les photos des travaux finis se trouvent page 11 à 17 pour faciliter le choix d'un modèle.

2 Chaque modèle est présenté sur une double page qui donne une photo de l'endroit et une photo de l'envers du travail, un schéma qui donne le nombre de paires de fuseaux et le sens du travail, un carton.

3 Tous les modèles sont présentés dans le même ordre:

1-a: vue de l'endroit

1-b: vue de l'envers

1-c: sens du travail

1-d: nombre de paires de fuseaux

1-e: carton

4 La photo de l'envers permet une comparaison du travail avec le modèle pendant la réalisation de la dentelle.

5 Tous les modèles sont réalisés avec du fil égyptien 170; quand un fil plus gros est nécessaire, du fil à coudre DMC Retors d'Alsace no. 50 est utilisé.

6 Sur les schémas le sens du travail est indiqué par des flèches et le nombre de paires de fuseaux nécessaire pour chaque partie est désigné par un nombre.

Exemple: 5 = 5 paires ou 10 fuseaux.

La paire de fil gros est désignée par C.

Exemple: 6 + C Signifie 6 paires de fuseaux plus une paire de gros fil. 0.5 C signifie un seul gros fil.

Le lacet est désigné par R.

Exemple: R5 signifie lacet de 5 paires.

7 Tous les cartons sont grandeur nature.

Finished pieces
(actual size)

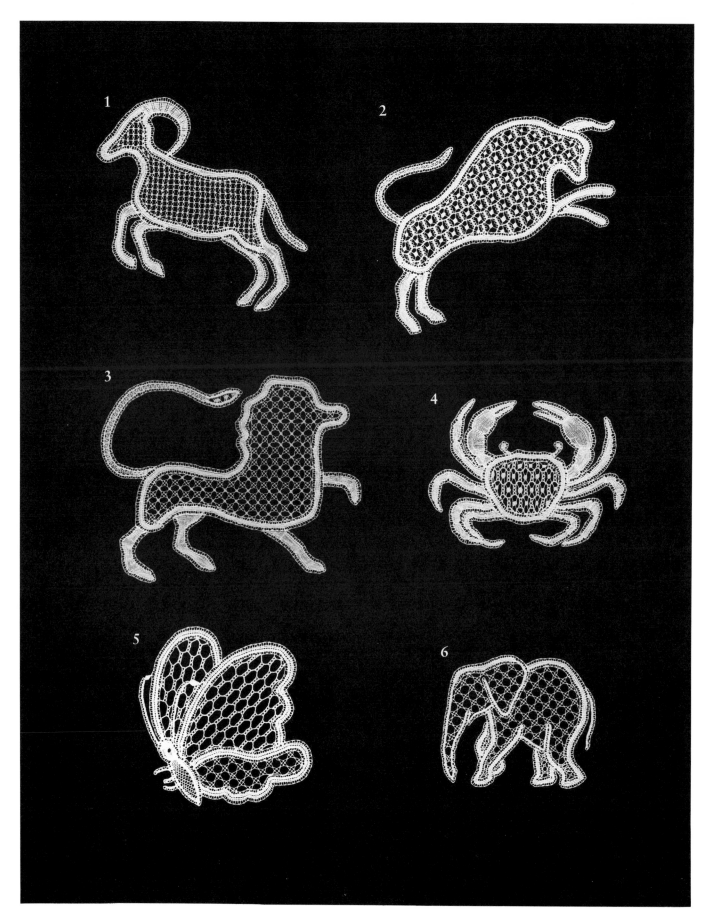

23 24 25 26 27 28

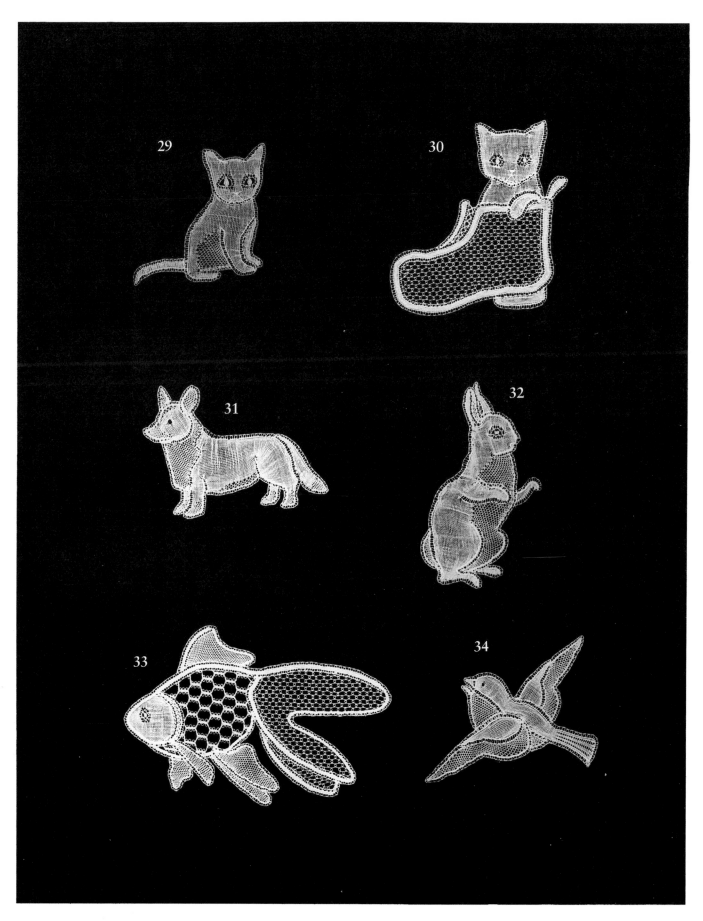

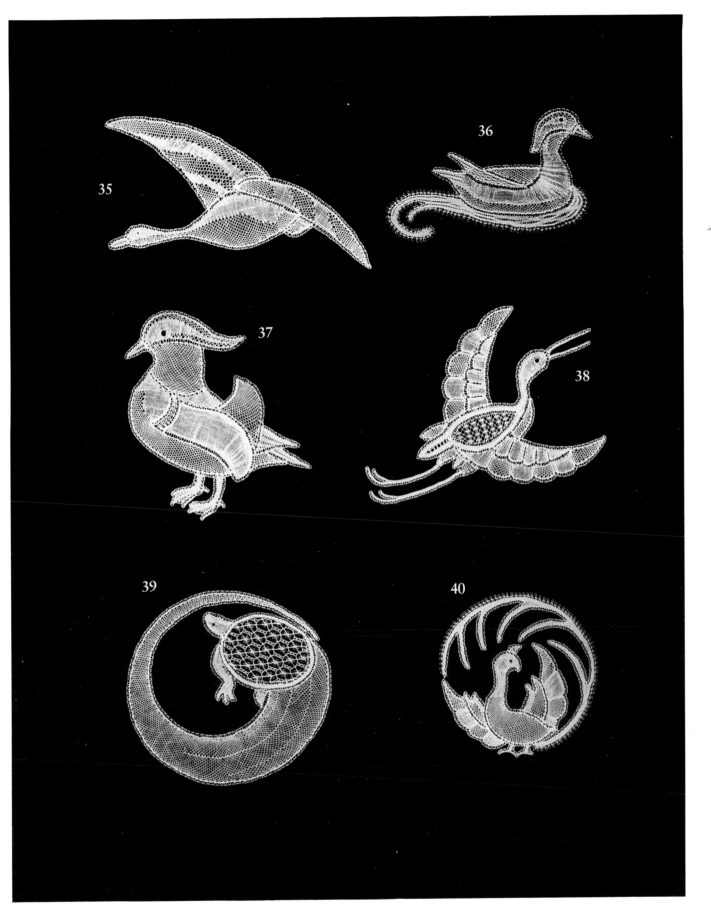

Saikoh Takano's patterns

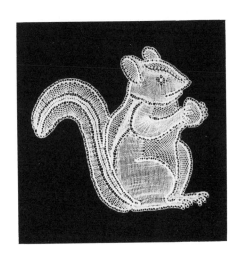

1 Capricorn

Start at the hoof (1) with six pairs and the coarse pair. Gradually add four pairs, and a coarse pair to divide into two. At the top of the head take out the inner coarse pair, and join and make the horn.

Fig. 1a   right side

Fig. 1c   working order

Am Huf (1) mit sechs Paaren und einem dicken Paar beginnen. Nach und nach vier Paare und ein dickes Paar hinzufügen, um zwei Teile zu erhalten; am Scheitel das innere Paar mit dickem Faden herausnehmen, und alle Paare für das Horn vereinen.

Begin bij de hoef (1) met zes paar en een dik paar. Voeg geleidelijk vier paar toe, en een dik paar; verdeel in tweeën bovenaan de kop; leg het binnenste dikke paar uit, voeg alles samen en klos de hoorn.

Commencer au sabot (1) avec 6 p. et une p. de gros fil. Ajouter peu à peu 4 p. et une p. de gros fil. Partager en 2 au sommet de la tête, retirer la p. interne de gros fil. Réunir tous les fuseaux pour faire la corne.

Fig. 1b   wrong side

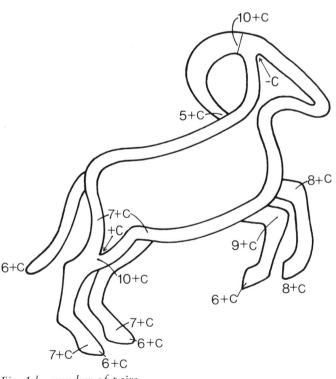

Fig. 1d   number of pairs

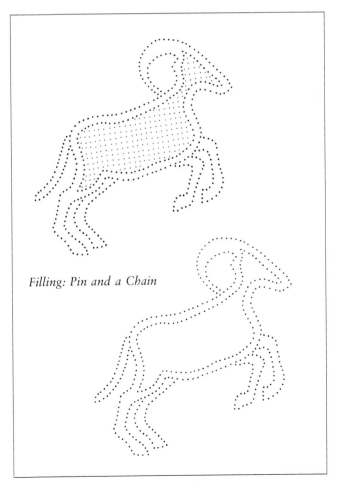

Filling: Pin and a Chain

Fig. 1e   prickings

21

2 Taurus

Work the outline, starting with six pairs and the coarse pair, add one pair on the next row.

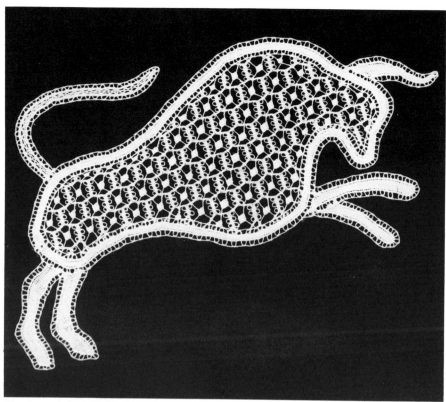

Fig. 2a   right side

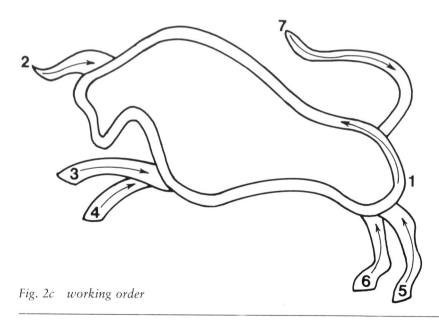

Fig. 2c   working order

Die Umrandung klöppeln, wobei man mit sechs Paaren und einem Paar mit dicken Garn beginnt; in der folgenden Reihe ein Paar hinzufügen.

Klos de omtrek, beginnend met zes paar en het dikke paar, leg op de volgende rij één paar bij.

Commencer le lacet contour avec 6 p. et la p. de gros fil. Au rang suivant ajouter 1 p.

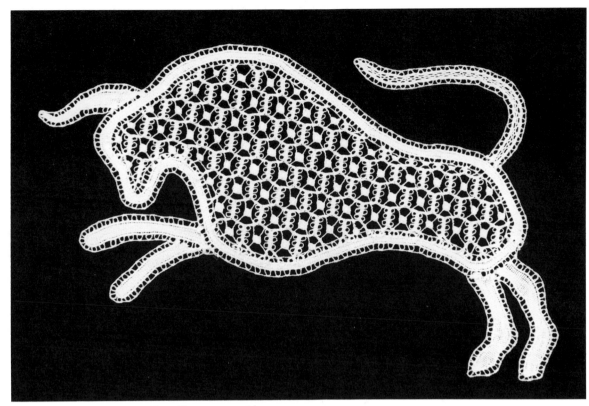

Fig. 2b   wrong side

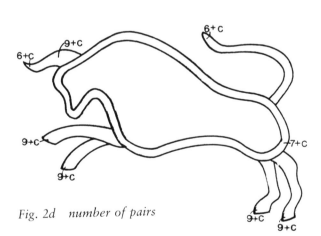

Fig. 2d   number of pairs

Fig. 2e   prickings

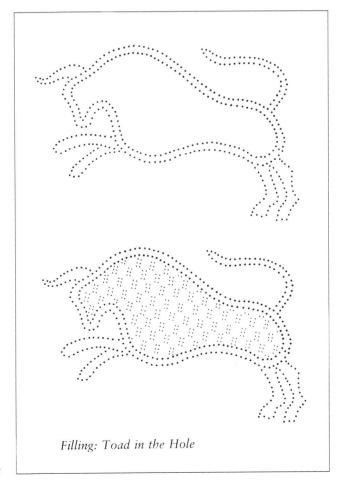

Filling: Toad in the Hole

23

3 Leo

Using 10 pairs at the top of the
tail, work a five-pair rib in each
direction. Where the ribs meet,
weave in a coarse pair, gradually
reducing to seven pairs and a
coarse pair. Fill in with Italian
filling at the tail.

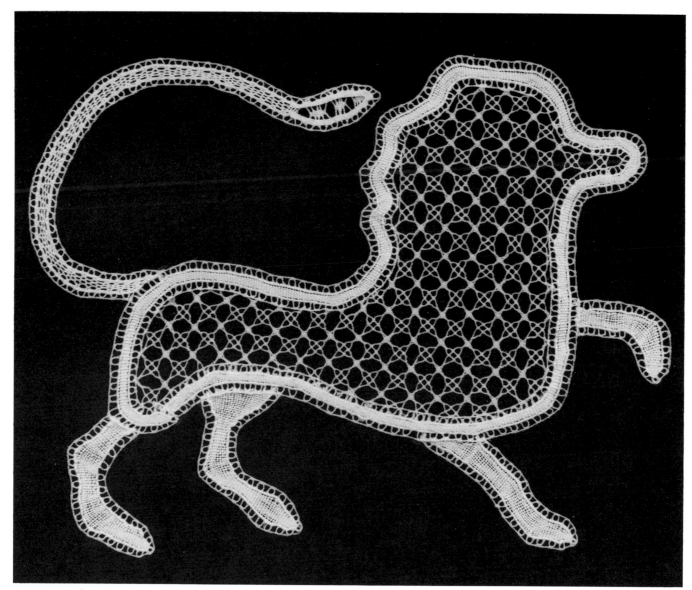

Fig. 3a   right side

Für die Schwanzspitze braucht man zehn
Paare, um eine Fünf-Paar-Rippe an beiden
Seiten zu klöppeln. Am Treffpunkt beider
Rippen ein Paar mit dickem Faden
einhäkeln, und die Anzahl der Paare nach
und nach auf sieben Paare und ein Paar
mit dicken Faden verringern.

Klos met 10 paar aan de punt van de
staart in beide richtingen een 5-parige rib.
Weef waar de ribjes samen komen, een
dik paar in, verminder geleidelijk tot
zeven paar en een dik paar. Vul de
staartpunt met Italian.

Prendre 10 p. à l'extrémité de la queue et
travailler le lacet contour de chaque côté
avec 5 p. Ajouter 1 p. de gros fil quand
on réunit tous les fuseaux et réduire peu à
peu à 7 p. et la p. de gros fil. Utiliser le
fond 'Italian' pour la queue.

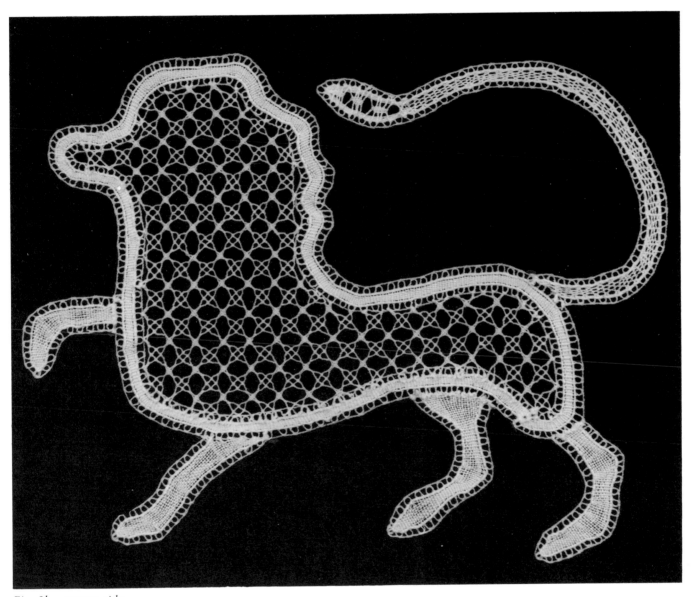

Fig. 3b   wrong side

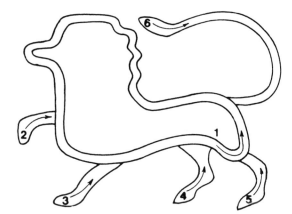

Fig. 3c   working order

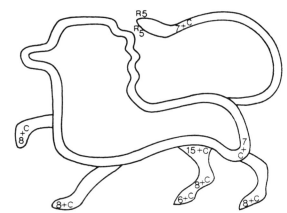

Fig. 3d   number of pairs

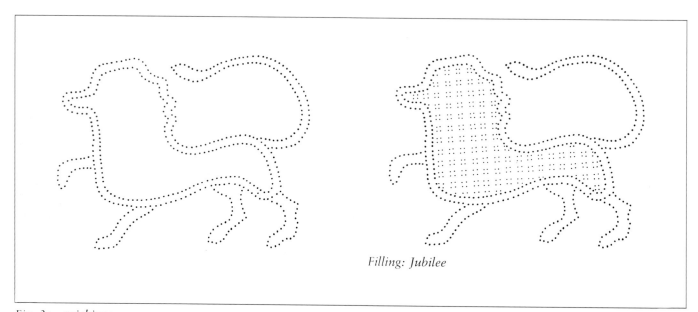

Filling: Jubilee

Fig. 3e   prickings

4 Cancer

Make the left tip of the claw, then
leave the threads to one side.
Make the right tip of the claw;
take out the inner coarse threads,
and continue to work across all
the remaining pairs.

Fig. 4a right side

Die linke Spitze der Zange klöppeln, dann
alle Fäden an einer Seite liegen lassen.
Nach Vollendung der rechten Zange das
Innenpaar mit dickem Faden
herausnehmen, und mit allen restlichen
Paaren klöppeln.

Klos de linker punt van de schaar, leg dan
de klossen opzij. Klos de rechter
schaarpunt, leg de binnenste dikke draden
uit, en klos verder met alle overgebleven
paren.

Commencer par la partie gauche de la
pince, laisser en attente. Faire la partie
droite de la pince. Retirer le gros fil
interne et continuer le travail avec les
paires restantes.

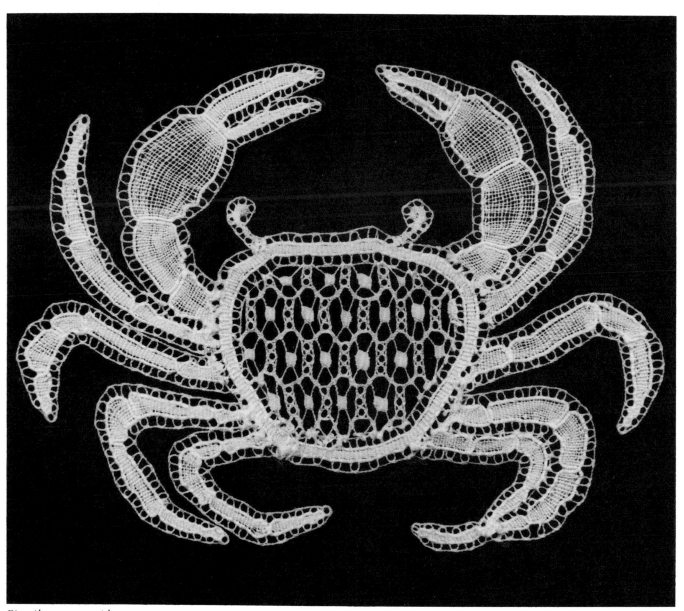

Fig. 4b   wrong side

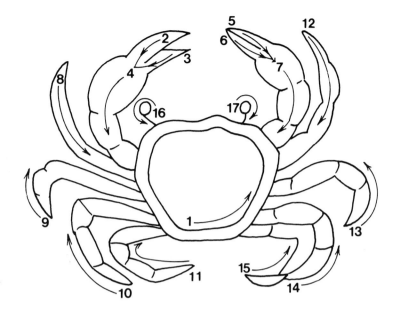

Fig. 4c   working order

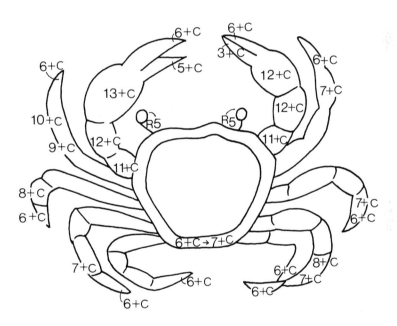

Fig. 4d   number of pairs

Filling: Toad in the Hole (variation 1)

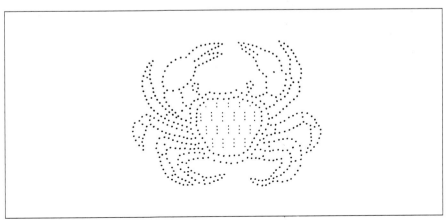

Fig. 4e   pricking

5 Butterfly (1)

Twist the runner and two passives
twice at the eye, and twist the
runner again on the next row. For
each antenna sew two pairs into
the wing, make the leaves and add
three pairs to make the rib.

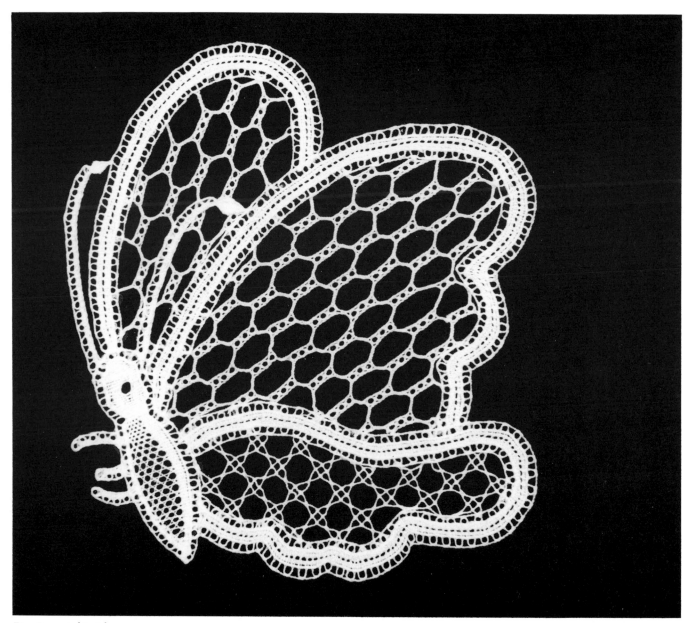

Fig. 5a   right side

Das Laufpaar und zwei Rißpaare am Auge
zweimal, und das Laufpaar nochmals in
der folgenden Reihe drehen. Für jeden
Fühler am Flügel zwei Paare einhäkeln,
der Formschlag klöppeln und drei Paare
für die Rippe hinzufügen.

Draai de lopers en twee hangende paren
bij het oog twee keer, en draai de lopers
op de volgende rij nog eens. Hang voor
elke voelspriet twee paar in de vleugel,
klos de blaadjes en leg drie paar in voor
de rib.

2 torsions sur les voyageurs et 2 passives
pour l'oeil, et tordre encore les voyageurs
au rang suivant. Pour chaque antenne,
accrocher 2 p. sur l'aile, faire un point
d'esprit et ajouter 3 p. pour continuer en
lacet contour.

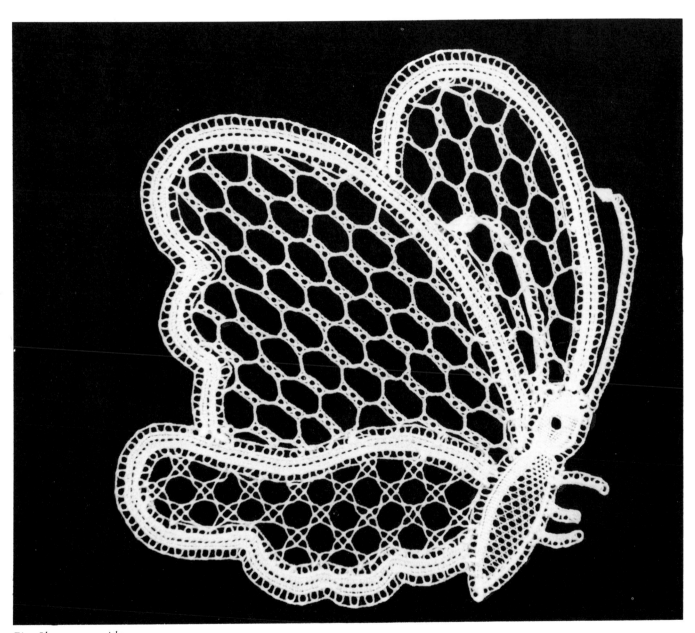

Fig. 5b   wrong side

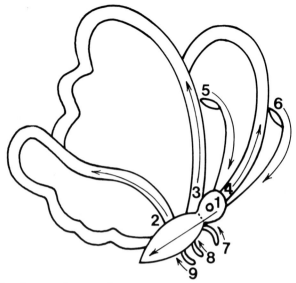

Fig. 5c   *working order*

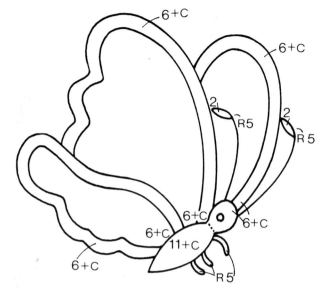

Fig. 5d   *number of pairs*

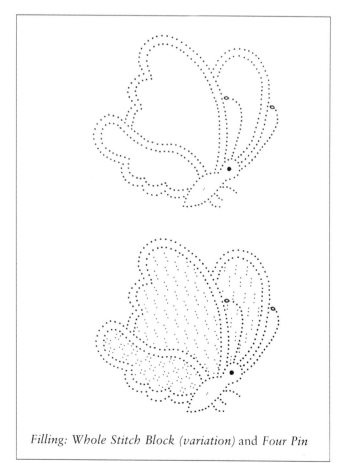

Filling: *Whole Stitch Block (variation)* and *Four Pin*

Fig. 5e   *prickings*

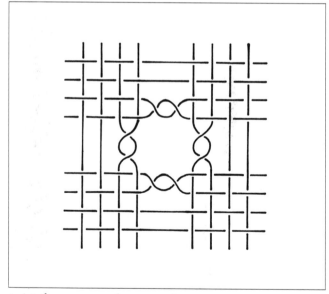

twist the runner and two passives
twice at the eye, and twist the runner
again on the next row

6 Elephant

Make the rib to the top of the
ear; weave in a coarse pair; make
whole stitch braid to the forehead;
take out the coarse pair and
change to rib again.

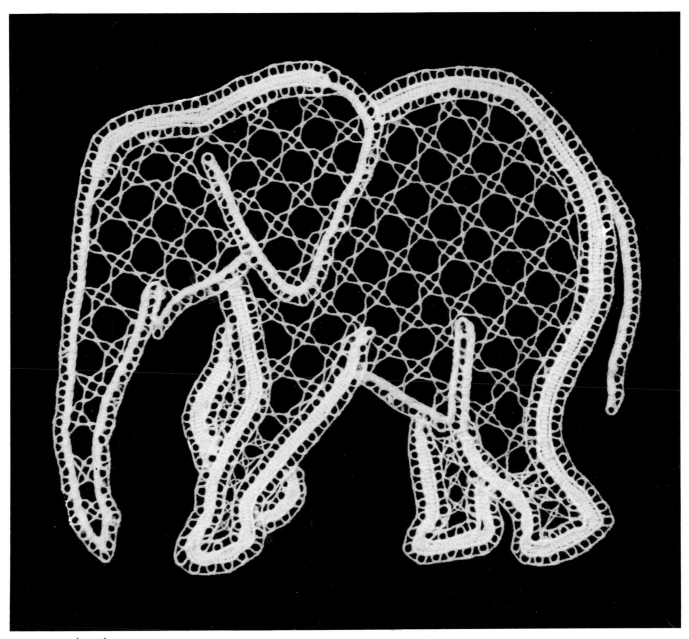

Fig. 6a right side

Die Rippe am Ohr nach oben klöppeln;
ein Paar mit dickem Faden einhäkeln; am
vorderen Kopf das Leinenschlag-Band
klöppeln; den dicken Faden herausnehmen
und wieder eine Rippe bilden.

Klos de rib tot de bovenkant van het oor;
weef een dik paar in; klos een linnenslag
bandje tot het voorhoofd; leg de dikke
draad weer uit en ga verder met een rib.

Faire le lacet contour à la pointe de
l'oreille. Ajouter le gros fil, faire un lacet
toilé 2 bords pour le crâne, retirer le gros
fil et continuer en lacet contour.

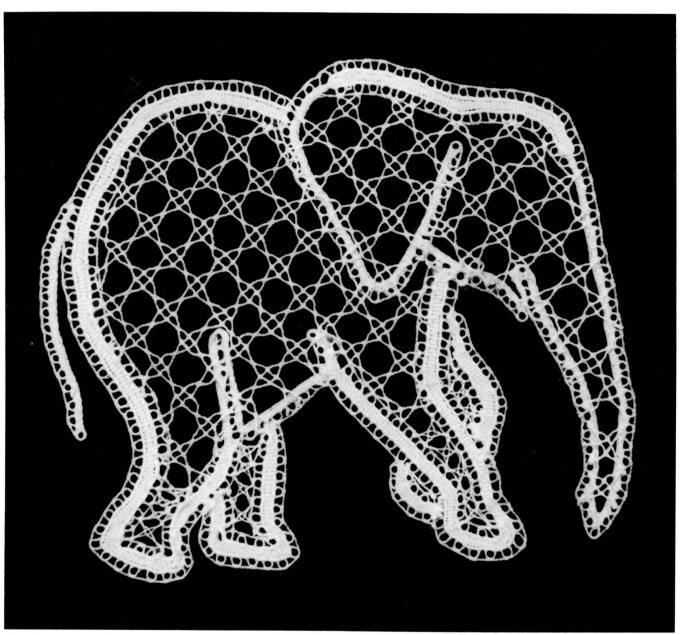

Fig. 6b   wrong side

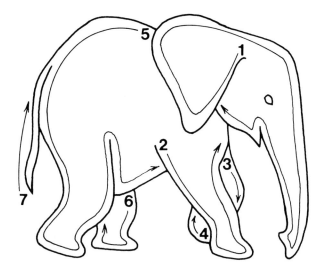

Fig. 6c   working order

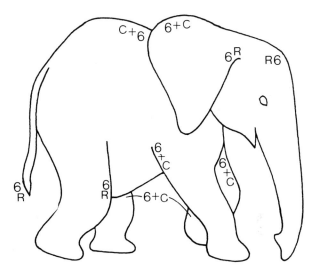

Fig. 6d   number of pairs

Filling: Four Pin

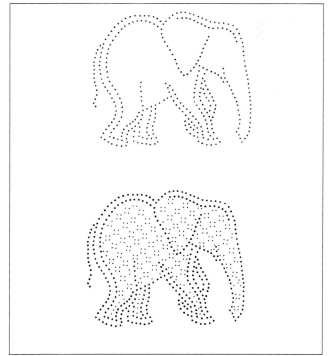

Fig. 6e   prickings

7 Butterfly (2)

For each antenna set up a pin,
hang two pairs open, twisting
each pair twice; make the leaf,
add two pairs and change to rib.
Join the two ribs together to make
the body.

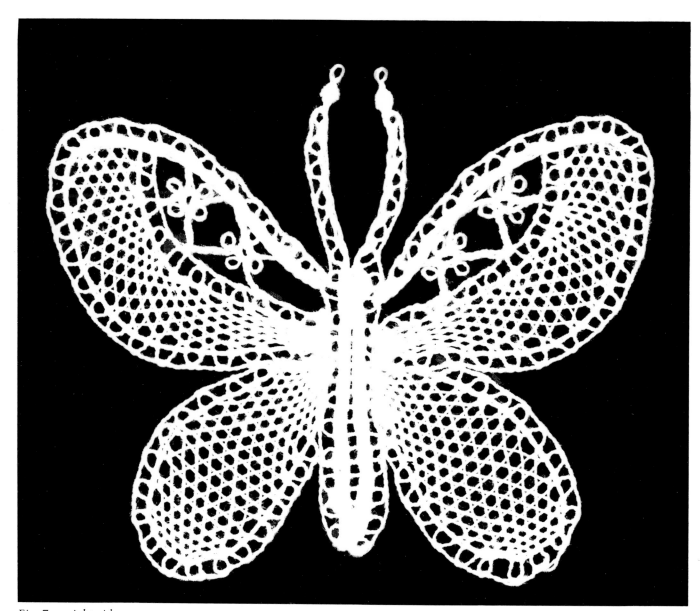

Fig. 7a   right side

Für jeden Fühler an eine Nadel zwei Paare
offen einhängen, und jedes Paar zweimal
drehen; den Formschlag klöppeln, zwei
Paare hinzufügen und zur Rippe
übergehen. Beide Rippen für den Körper
vereinen.

Zet voor elke voelspriet een speld, hang
twee paar open, elk paar twee maal
gedraaid; klos het blaadje, leg twee paar
in en ga verder in rib. Voeg de twee ribjes
samen om het lijf te klossen.

Commencer chaque antenne en plaçant 2
p. à cheval sur une épingle, 2 torsions de
chaque côté, faire un point d'esprit et
ajouter 2 paires pour continuer en lacet
contour. Les fuseaux des 2 antennes se
regroupent pour former le corps.

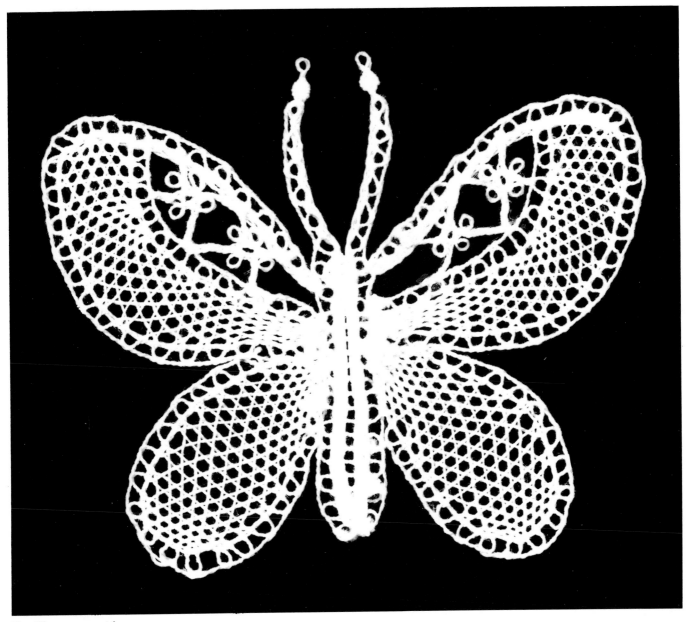

Fig. 7b   wrong side

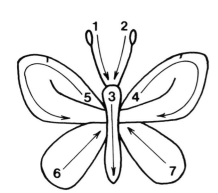

Fig. 7c   working order

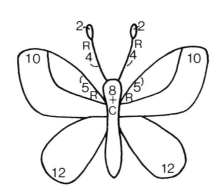

Fig. 7d   number of pairs

Filling: Blossom

Fig. 7e   pricking

8 Ladybird

At (6) sew eight pairs into the base of the shell; work half stitch, remembering to work one whole stitch and twist at the central passive on each row.

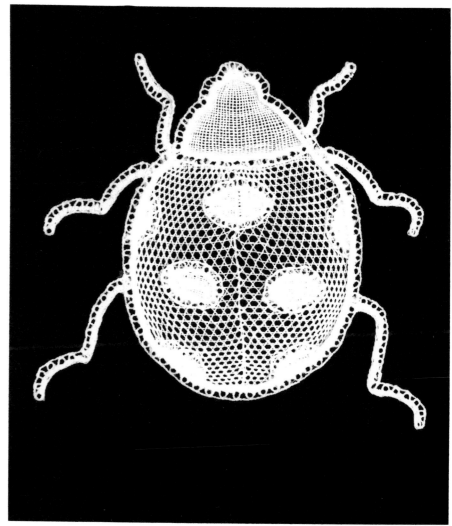

Fig. 8a right side

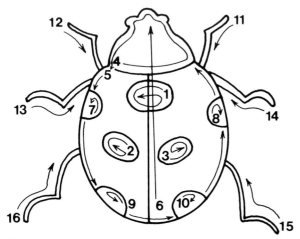

Fig. 8c working order

Bei Punkt (6) acht Paare unten am Panzer einhäkeln; im Halbstich klöppeln, wobei jedoch in jeder Reihe ein Ganzschlag mit den mittleren Rißpaaren auszuführen ist.

Hang bij (6) acht paar in de basis van het schild; klos netslag, en denk eraan één linnenslag en draai te klossen bij het middelste hangende paar op elke rij.

Sur 6, accrocher 8 paires pour la partie inférieure des 2 ailes. Faire en pt simple, sans oublier de marquer la séparation par un pt dble au milieu, à chaque rang.

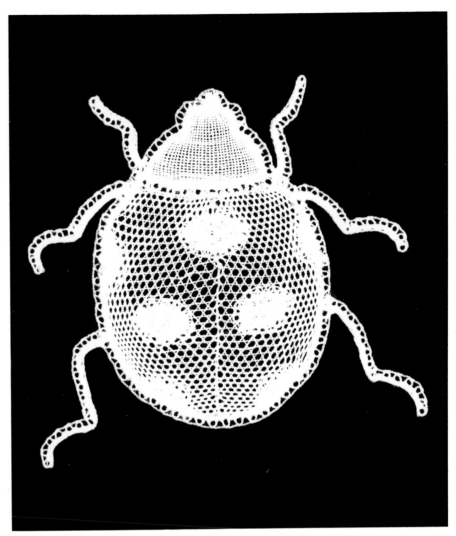

Fig. 8b   wrong side

Fig. 8d   number of pairs

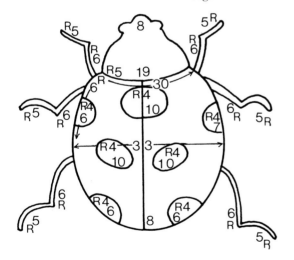

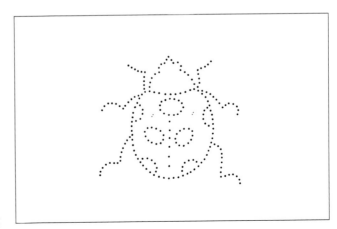

Fig. 8e   pricking

39

9 Bee

To make the windows in the
lower abdomen, work one twist
for the runner and two for each
passive.

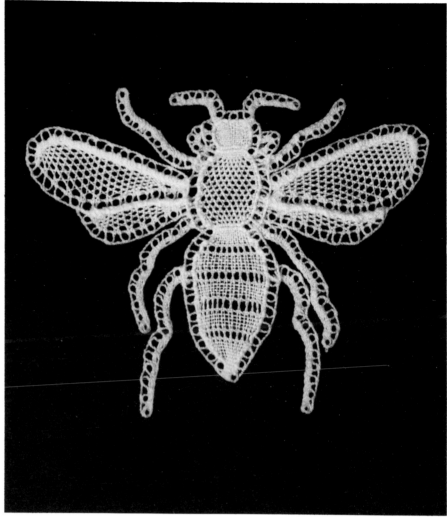

Fig. 9a   right side

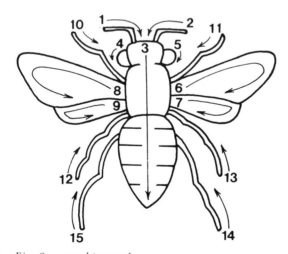

Fig. 9c   working order

Für die Lochreihe im unteren Körperteil
wird das Laufpaar einmal und jedes
Rißpaar zweimal gedreht.

Klos in het onderlijf één draai voor de
loper en twee voor ieder hangend paar,
voor de open luchtjes.

Les rayures du corps se font avec l torsion
des voyageurs et 2 torsions sur chaque
passives.

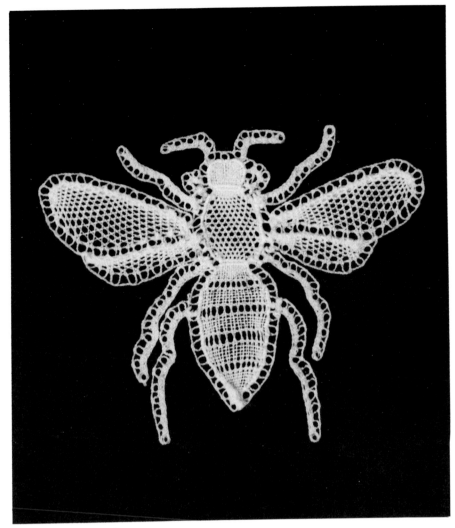

Fig. 9b   wrong side

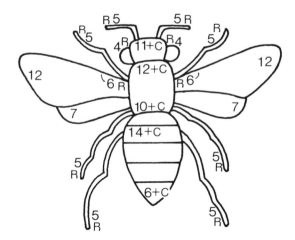

Fig. 9d   number of pairs

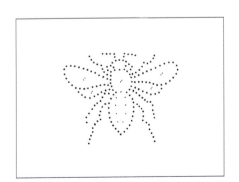

Fig. 9e   pricking

10 Frog

Make the head, increase to 14
pairs and a coarse pair; make the
eye then leave the threads to one
side after setting up the pin at the
end of the mouth. Make the lower
jaw, then work across all the
threads to make the body.

Fig. 10a   right side

Den Kopf klöppeln, wobei bis zu 14
Paaren und ein Paar mit dickem Faden
zugenommen wird; das Auge beenden,
und am Ende des Mauls eine Nadel
stecken und alle Fäden auf einer Seite
liegen lassen. Den Unterkiefer klöppeln,
dann für den Körper alle Paare
werwenden.

Klos de kop, vermeerder tot 14 paar en
een dik paar; klos het oog, zet een speld
aan het eind van de bek en leg de klossen
opzij. Klos de onderkaak, werk dan voor
het lijf door alle paren.

Commencer par la tête et arriver à 14 p.
+ 1 p. gros fil . Faire l'oeil, laisser les fils
en attente après avoir mis une épingle sur
la fin de la bouche. Faire la mâchoire
inféreure et reprendre tous les fils pour le
corps.

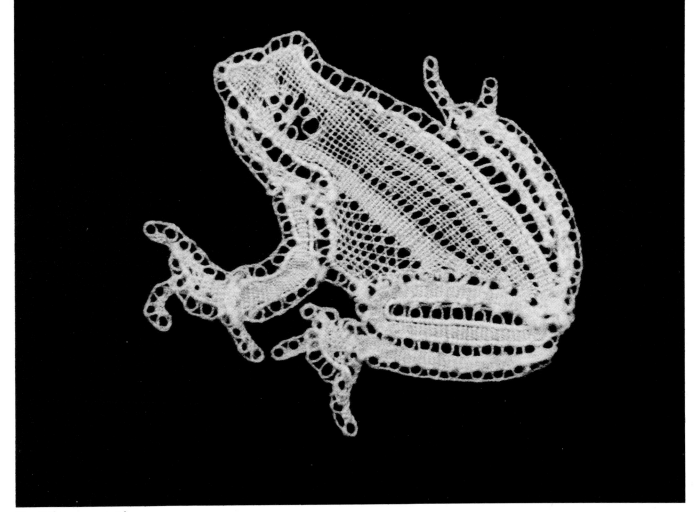

Fig. 10b   wrong side

Fig. 10c   working order

Fig. 10d   number of pairs

Fig. 10e   pricking

43

11 Snail

Work whole stitch braid across the end of the shell, changing to rib at the outer edge. Make the left feeler (3), leaving the threads to one side while making the other feeler (4), and the top part of the head; then join to continue the head and body.

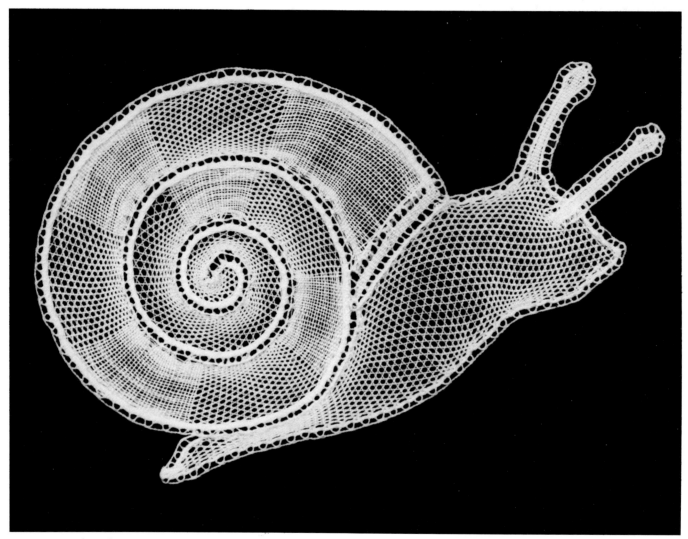

Fig. 11a right side

Das Leinenschlagband am Ende des Schneckenhauses wird am äußeren Rand wie eine Rippe geklöppelt. Nach dem linken Fühler (3) läßt man beim Klöppeln des rechten Fühlers (4) die Fäden an einer Seite oben am Kopf liegen; Kopf und Körper mit allen Paaren ausführen.

Klos langs het eind van het huis een linnenslagbandje, ga aan de buitenkant over in rib. Klos de voelspriet (3), leg de klossen opzij, maak de andere voelspriet en de bovenkant van de kop; voeg dan samen voor de rest van de kop en het lijf.

Pour marquer l'arrêt de la coquille faire un lacet toilé 2 bords, continuer le colimaçon en lacet contour. Faire la corne gauche (3), laisser les fils en attente. Faire la corne droite (4) et le sommet de la tête avant d'ajouter les paires de la corne gauche pour travailler la suite avec tous les fuseaux.

44

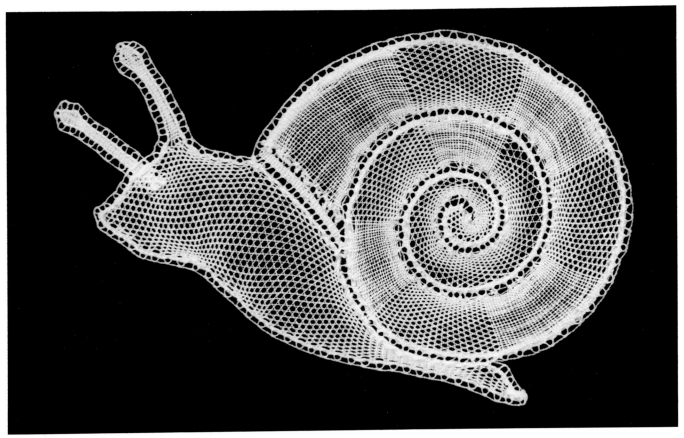

Fig. 11b   wrong side

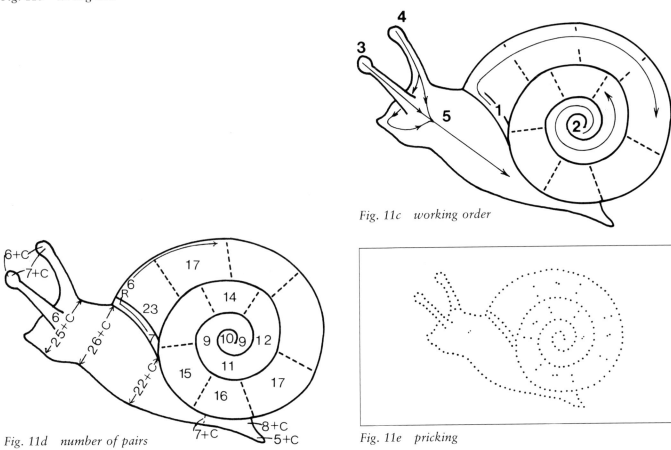

Fig. 11c   working order

Fig. 11d   number of pairs

Fig. 11e   pricking

12 Shrike

Put four pins at the eye between the passive pairs, to keep them apart, then continue in half stitch. Make one whole stitch and twist with a central passive pair at the centre of the belly. The shrike eats small animals such as frogs and insects; after killing her prey, she stores them on a branch for her winter food.

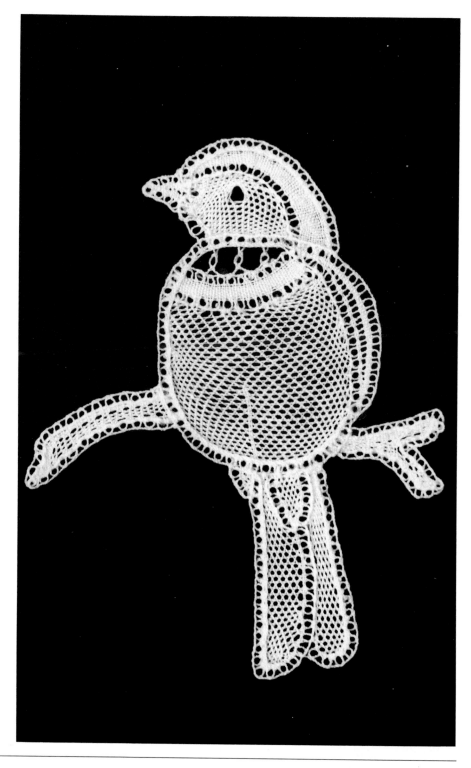

Fig. 12a   right side

Am Auge zwischen die Rißpaare vier Nadeln stecken, um sie voneinander zu trennen, dann im Halbschlag fortfahren. In der Bauchmitte einen Ganzschlag mit einem mittleren Rißpaar klöppeln. Der Würger frißt kleine Tiere, wie Frösche und Insekten; nachdem er seine Beute getötet hat, hält er sie für den Winter auf einem Ast auf Vorrat.

Zet bij het oog vier spelden tussen de hangende paren, om die uit elkaar te houden, ga door in netslag. Klos één linnenslag en draai met een hangend paar in het midden van de buik. De Klauwier eet kleine dieren als kikkers en insecten; na de prooi gedood te hebben, bewaart hij die op een tak voor zijn wintervoorraad.

Mettre 4 épingles entre les passives pour ajourer l'oeil et continuer en point simple. Marquer le milieu du corps par un point dble sur la partie centrale du ventre. La pie-grièche mange de petits animaux tels les grenouilles et les insectes. Elle stocke ses proies tuées sur une branche pour l'hiver.

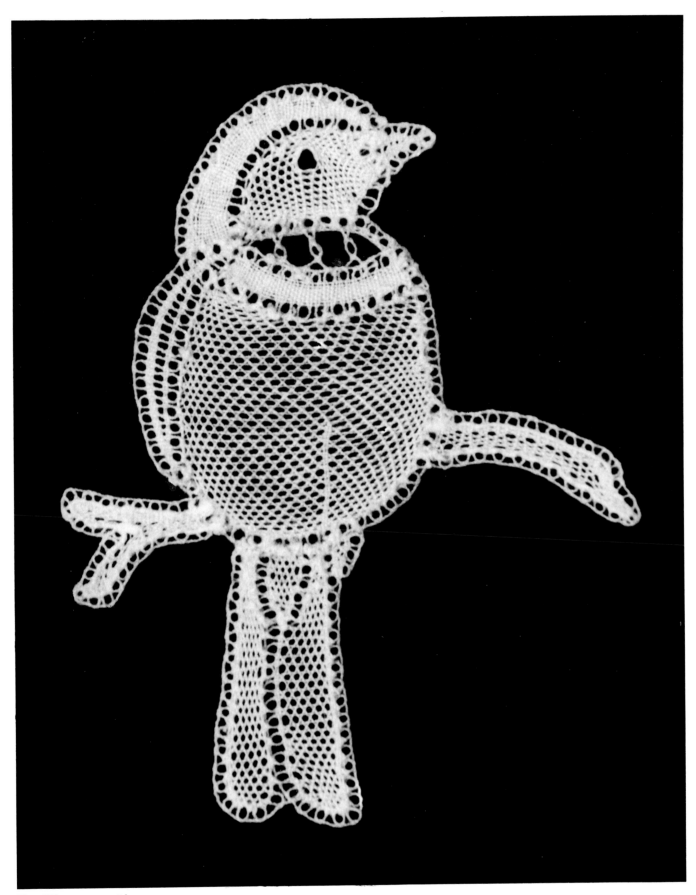

Fig. 12b   wrong side

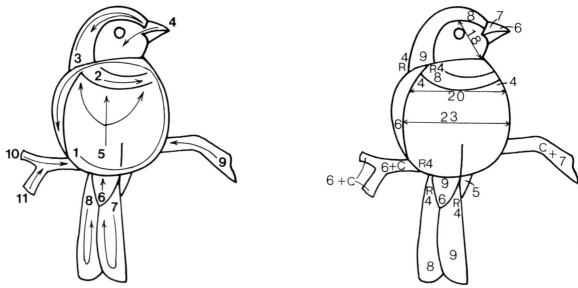

Fig. 12c   working order

Fig. 12d   number of pairs

Fig. 12e   pricking

Filling: Pin and a Stitch

48

13 Mouse

Cross the passives from the head and the right paw, using each of the latter pairs as a new runner pair, then as a new passive pair after the whole stitch with the edge pair.

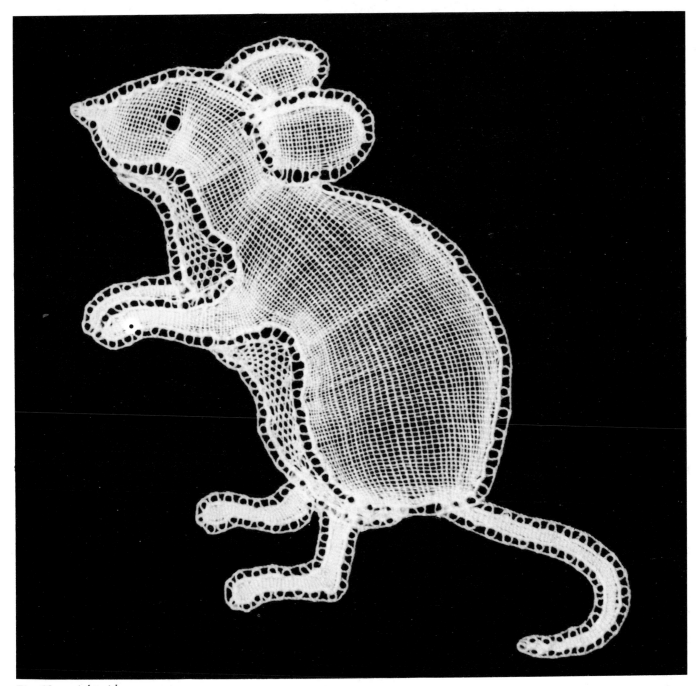

Fig. 13a   right side

Die Rißpaare von Kopf und rechter Pfote kreuzen, wobei die Paare der Pfote als neues Laufpaar, dann nach dem Leinenschlag mit dem Randpaar als neues Rißpaar benutzt werden.

Werk de paren van de kop en de rechterpoot door elkaar; gebruik elk paar van de poot als nieuw looppaar, later als nieuw hangend paar na de linnenslag met het randpaar.

Croiser les passives de la tête et de la patte droite en utilisant chaque fois la dernière passive comme nouveau meneur puis ces paires redeviennent passives après avoir travaillé le point de bordure.

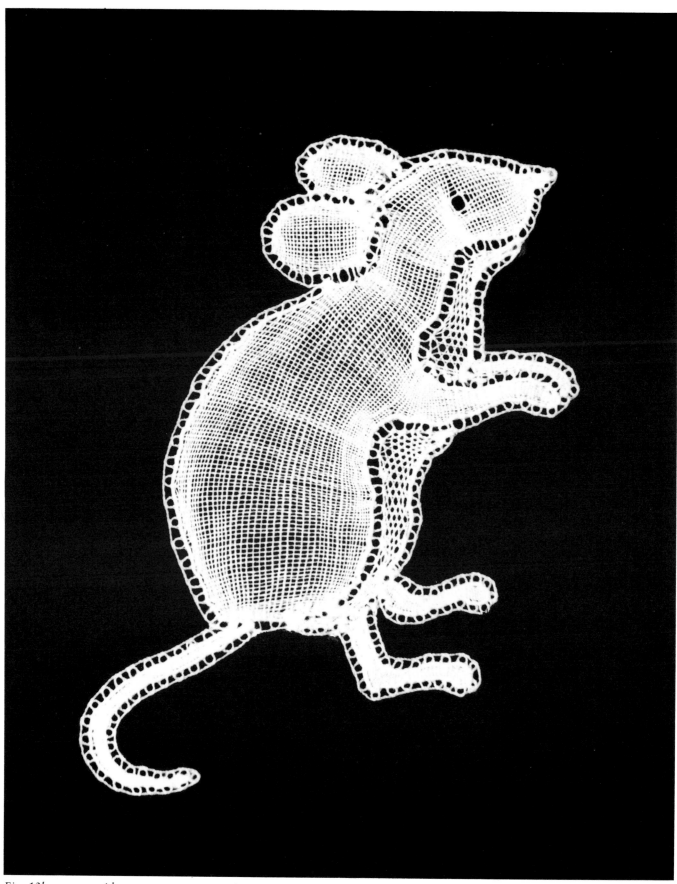

Fig. 13b   wrong side

50

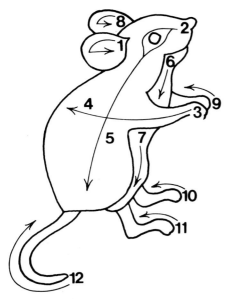

Fig. 13c   working order

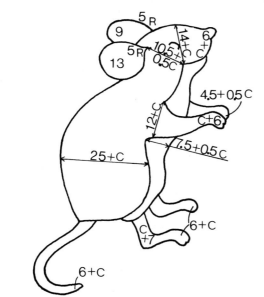

Fig. 13d   number of pairs

Fig. 13e   pricking

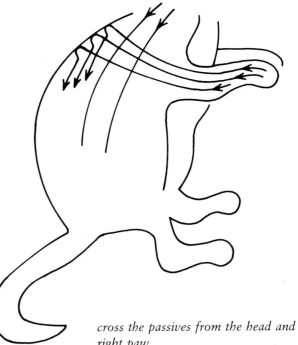

cross the passives from the head and right paw

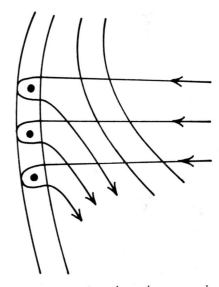

weaving passives through one another

14 Goldfish

Join the threads from the body,
and rib at the base of the tail.
Extra pairs are added in the tail
by setting up a pin to the left of a
passive pair; hang a new pair on
the pin, with the right-hand
thread over the passive to the
right (*see* Fig. 14*f*).

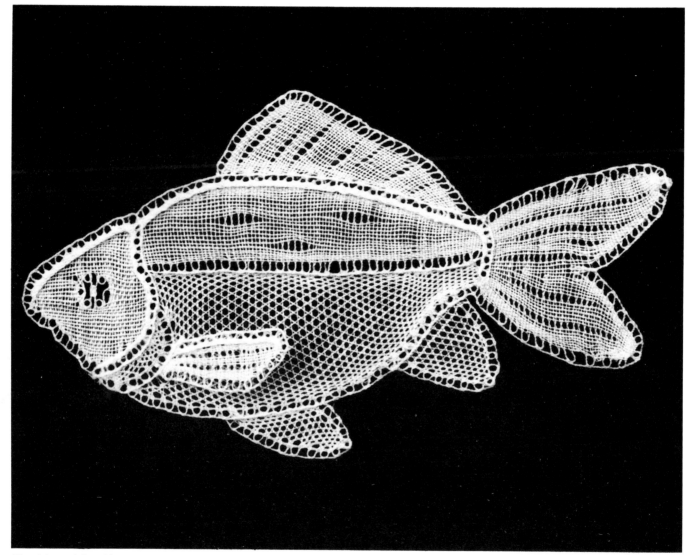

Fig. 14a   right side

Die vom Körper kommenden Paare
vereinen, und am Beginn des Schwanzes
eine Rippe klöppeln. Um die zusätzlichen
Paare für den Schwanz hinzuzufügen,
steckt man eine Nadel links von einem
Rißpaar; daran hängt man ein neues Paar,
wobei der rechte Faden nach rechts über
das Rißpaar gelegt wird (siehe Abb. *14-f*).

Voeg de paren van het lijf samen, en rib
de aanzet van de staart. Leg extra paren
in de staart in door een speld te zetten
links van een hangend paar; hang een
nieuw paar aan de speld, met de
rechterdraad over de hangende draad
ernaast. (*zie* fig 14f).

Accrocher les paires sur la tête. Faire le
lacet contour du corps en le tournant
pour marquer la queue (suivre flèche 4).
Accrocher de nouvelles paires pour la
queue. L'élargir en ajoutant des paires
internes: placer une épingle à gauche
d'une passive, y pendre une nouvelle paire
et croiser 2/3 (*voir* Fig. *14*f)

Fig. 14b   wrong side

Fig. 14c   working order

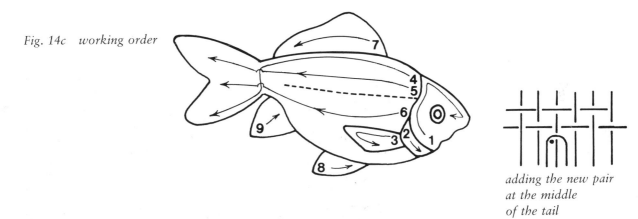

adding the new pair
at the middle
of the tail

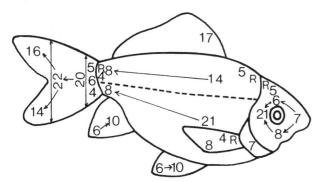

Fig. 14d   number of pairs

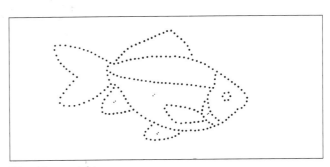

Fig. 14e   pricking

15 Kingfisher

Make the beak, reduce the
threads, cut off the coarse pair,
roll up across the base of the
beak, then make the head.

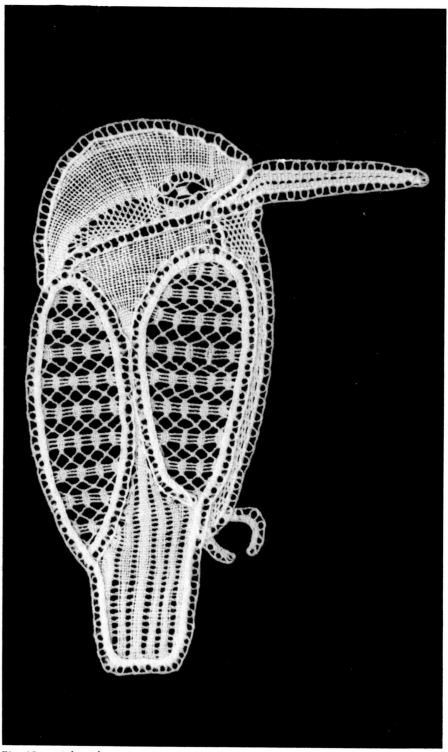

Fig. 15a   right side

Nach dem Schnabel die Fäden reduzieren,
das Paar mit dem dicken Faden
abschneiden, an der Schnabelbasis eine
Rolle bilden, und den Kopf klöppeln.

Klos de snavel, verminder het aantal
klossen, knip het dikke paar af, rol langs
de onderkant van de snavel, klos dan de
kop.

Faire le bec, réduire les paires, couper le
gros fil. Tordre en botte et remonter le
long de la base du bec pour reprendre la
tête en pointe.

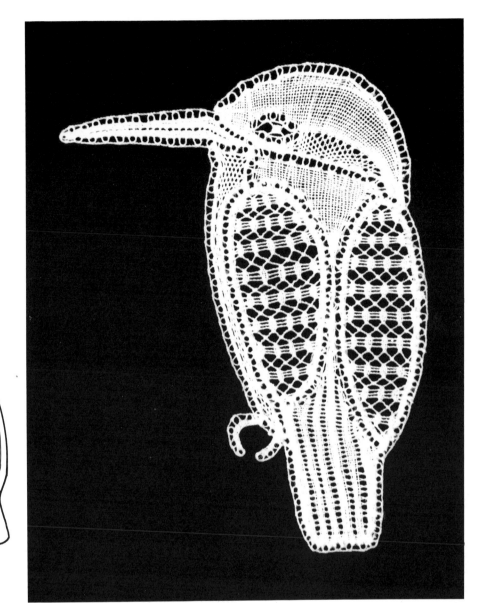

Fig. 15b   wrong side

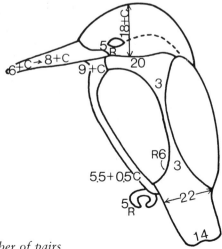

Fig. 15c   working order

Filling: Italian

Fig. 15d   number of pairs

Fig. 15e   pricking

55

16 Otter

Cross the passives from the body through the passives from the right-front paw, and work each pair towards the chest; work edge stitch and whole stitch with the first passive, tie them and cut off.

Fig. 16a   right side

Die Rißpaare des Körpers durchlaufen die Rißpaare der rechten Vorderpfote, um die Brust auszuführen; mit dem ersten Rißpaar einen Rand- und Leinenschlag klöppeln, knüpfen und abschneiden.

Werk de hangende paren van het lijf door die van de rechter voorpoot, en klos elk paar naar de borst; maak randslag en linnenslag met het eerste hangende paar, knoop en knip af.

Croiser les passives du corps avec les passives de la patte avant droite. Chaque paire travaille alors le poitrail. Faire le point de bordure, puis le point toile avec la première passive. Nouer. Couper.

Fig. 16b   wrong side

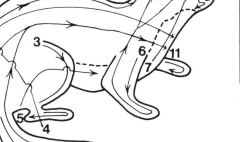

Fig. 16c   working order

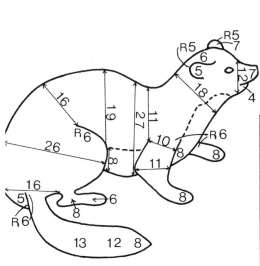

Fig. 16d   number of pairs

Fig. 16e   pricking

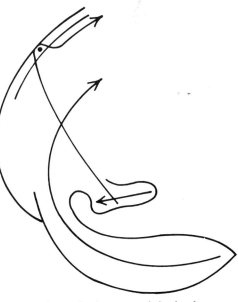

weave from the bottom of the back
paw through the body

17 Squirrel

Make the ear before finishing the
face; cross the passive threads
from the ear and face to finish (7).
Make the fingers and toes with rib
and rolling up to continue to
make the others.

Fig. 17a   right side

Bevor man das Gesicht zu Ende klöppelt,
macht man das Ohr; zum Abschluß die
Rißpaare von Ohr und Gesicht kreuzen (7).
Finger und Zehen mit einer Rippe
klöppeln und eine Rolle bilden, bevor die
anderen begonnen werden.

Klos het oor alvorens het gezicht af te
maken; eindig door de hangende paren
van oor en gezicht door elkaar te werken
(7). Klos een rib voor de vingers en tenen
en rol terug om de andere te maken.

Faire l'oreille d'abord, puis finir la tête en
croisant les passives de l'oreille avec celles
de la tête (7). Faire les griffes en lacet
contour. Ramener en botte pour aller de
l'une à l'autre.

Fig. 17c   working order

Fig. 17b   wrong side

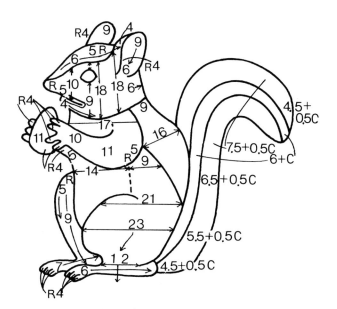

Fig. 17d   number of pairs

Fig. 17e   pricking

18 Swallow

It is said that if swallows make a
nest against the wall of your
house, or under the eaves of your
roof, your family will have good
fortune. This pattern reminds me
of the beautiful (but sad) story
'The Happy Prince'.

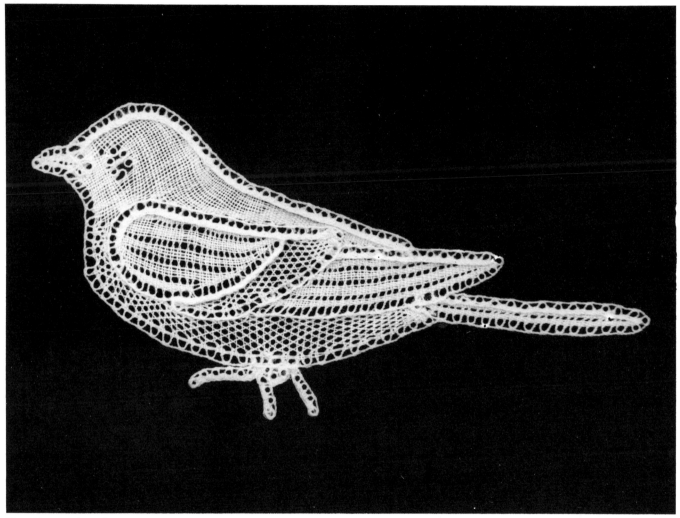

Fig. 18a   right side

Es heißt, daß ein Schwalbennest an der
Hausmauer oder unter dem Dachgiebel
dem Hausbesitzer Glück bringt. Dieses
Motiv erinnert mich an die schöne (aber
traurige) Geschichte 'Der glückliche
Prinz'.

Er wordt gezegd dat als zwaluwen tegen
de muur van Uw huis, of onder de
dakgoot een nest bouwen, dat Uw familie
geluk brengt. Dit patroon herinnert mij
aan het mooie (maar droevige) verhaal
'De Gelukkige Prins'.

On raconte que si une hirondelle construit
son nid sur le mur de votre maison, ou
sous l'auvent, c'est signe de bonne
fortune. Ce modèle me fait penser à la
très belle (et si triste) histoire du Prince
Joyeux.

Fig. 18b   wrong side

Fig. 18c   working order

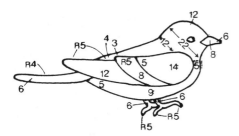

Fig. 18d   number of pairs

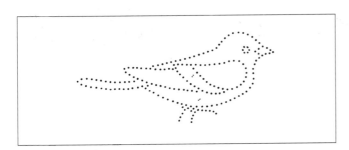

Fig. 18e   pricking

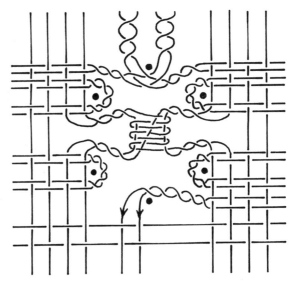

making the eye

19 Cicada

There are many kinds of cicada, which sing in many different ways. Make the body and wings separately, then sew them together.

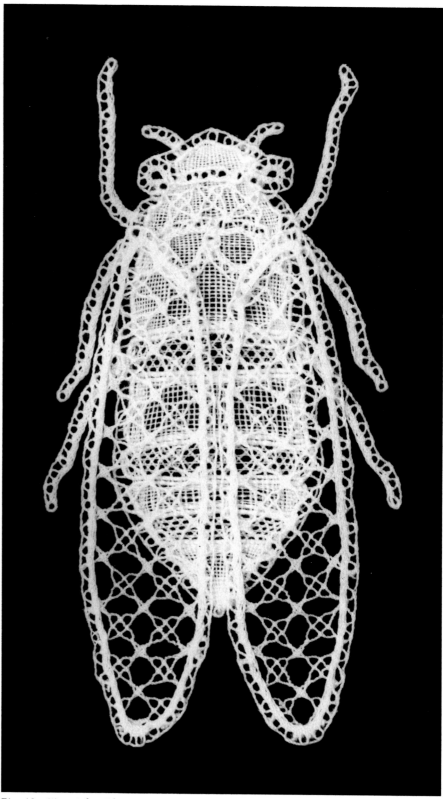

Fig. 19a (i)   right side

Es gibt viele Zikaden-Arten, die auf verschiedene Weise zirpen. Körper und Flügel werden getrennt geklöppelt und aneinander genäht.

Er zijn vele soorten Cicaden, die op verschillende manieren zingen. Klos lijf en vleugels apart, naai ze dan aan elkaar.

Il y a beaucoup de sortes de cigales qui toutes ont leur propre chant. Travailler les ailes et le corps séparément, puis les accrocher.

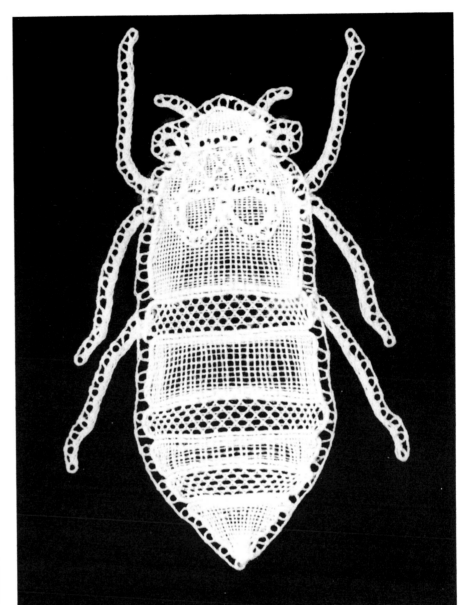

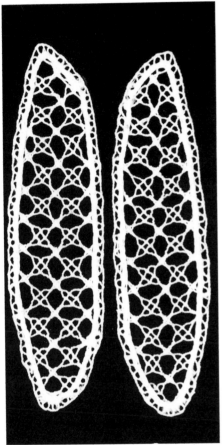

Figs 19a (ii) and (iii)   right side

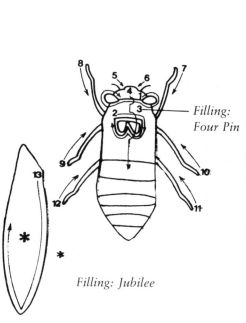

Filling: Four Pin

Filling: Jubilee

Fig. 19c   working order

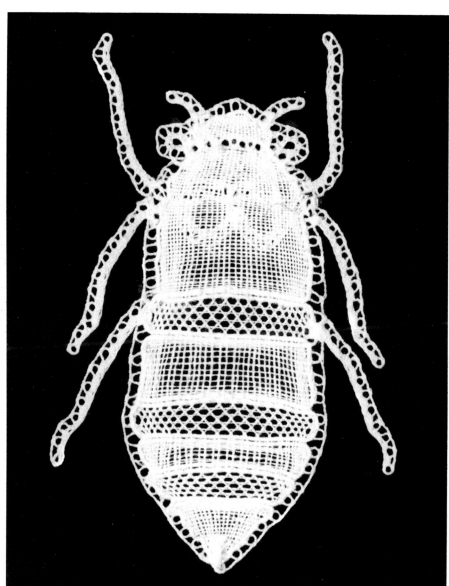

Fig. 19b   wrong side

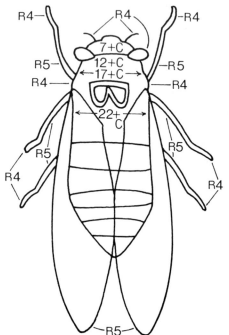

Fig. 19d   number of pairs

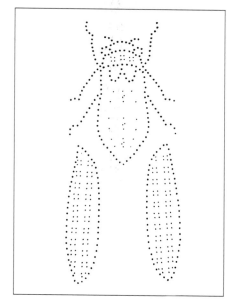

Fig. 19e   pricking

20 Fox

Foxes often feature in fables, but usually as 'baddies'. 'The Foxes' Wedding' is one of my favourite stories.

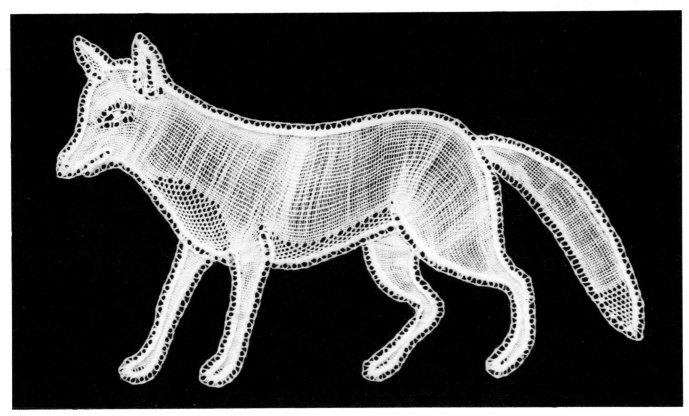

Fig. 20a   right side

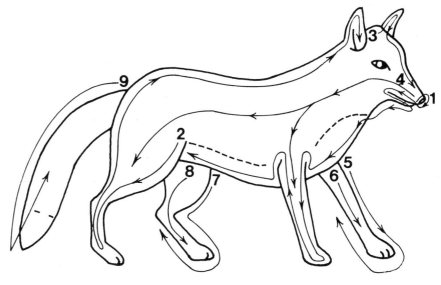

Fig. 20c   working order

Füchse kommen häufig in Fabeln vor, wo sie gewöhnliche die Rolle des Bösewichts spielen. Meine liebste Geschichte ist 'Die Fuchs-Hochzeit'.

Vossen komen veel in fabels voor, maar meestal als de slechterik. De 'Vossenbruiloft' is een van mijn lievelingsverhalen.

Le renard est souvent pris comme personnage de fable pour représenter les mauvais. Le mariage de Renard est mon conte préféré.

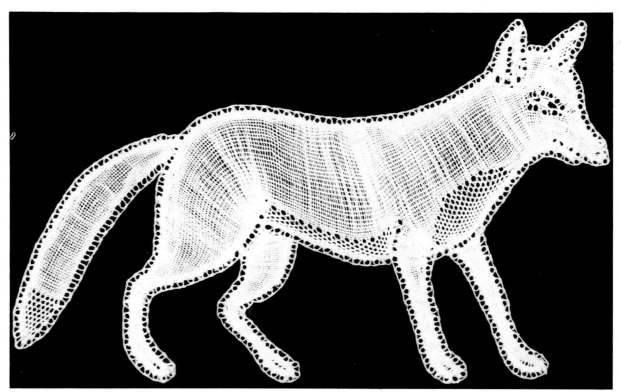

Fig. 20b   wrong side

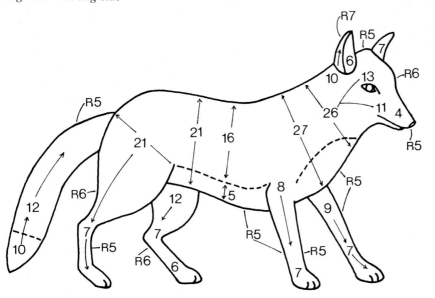

Fig. 20d   number of pairs

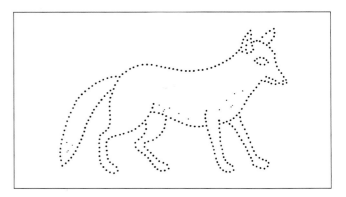

Fig. 20e   pricking

21 Owl

Make the toe as shown in the working order (9 and 10), crossing the passives.

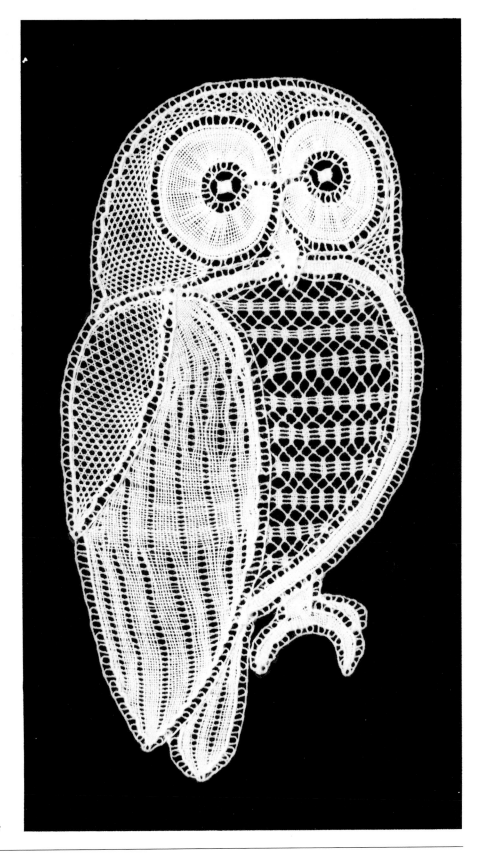

Fig. 21a   right side

Die Kralle wie auf der Zeichnung in der Reihenfolge (9 und 10) klöppeln, wobei die Rißpaare gekreuzt werden.

Klos de teen volgens de tekening van de werkvolgorde (9 en 10), werk de hangende paren dooreen.

Faire les serres selon l'ordre indiqué (9 et 10). Croiser les passives.

Fig. 21c   working order

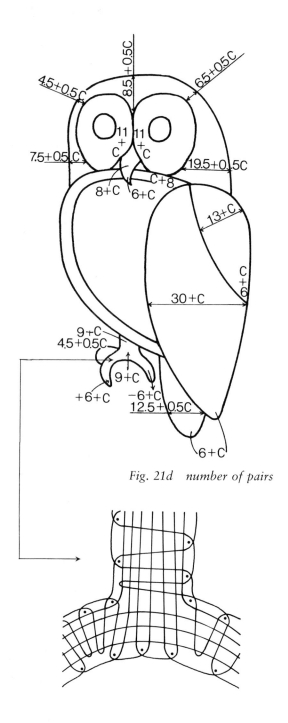

Fig. 21d   number of pairs

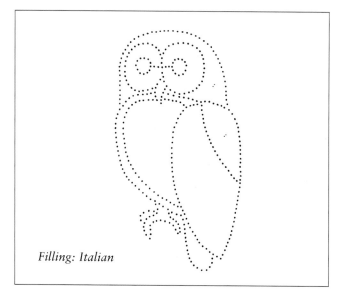

Filling: Italian

Fig. 21e   pricking

Fig. 21b   wrong side

22 Racoon

To work the lower foot (*11*) sew five pairs into the thigh, make a rib, roll up, make a rib, and sew the runner pair into the thigh several times; then make the second foot.

Fig. 22a   right side

Fü den vorderen Fuß (*11*) fünf neue Paare an der Hüfte einhäkeln, eine Rippe klöppeln, eine Rolle bilden, wieder eine Rippe klöppeln und das Laufpaar mehrere Male an der Hüfte einhäkeln; nun die zweite Zehe klöppen.

Hang voor de onderste poot (*11*) vijf paar in de dij, klos een rib, rol terug, klos een rib, en haak het looppaar een paar keer aan in de dij; klos dan de tweede teen.

Accrocher 5 paires sur la cuisse pour faire le lacet contour de la patte antérieure droite. Tordre en botte, faire un lacet contour et accrocher les voyageurs sur la cuisse plusieurs fois avant de faire la patte suivante.

Fig. 22b   wrong side

Fig. 22c   working order

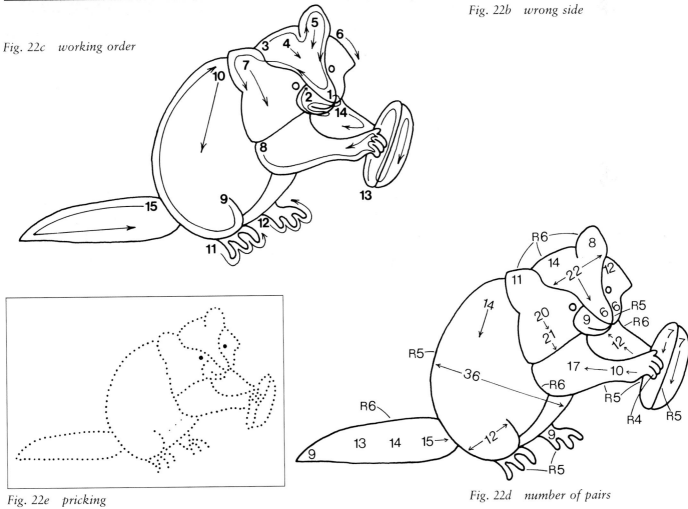

Fig. 22e   pricking

Fig. 22d   number of pairs

23 Penguin

Divide the passives into three parts at the eye, leaving two pairs for the centre section. Make a leaf with two centre pairs, working whole stitch to make the head and face, re-joining them at the base of the eye.

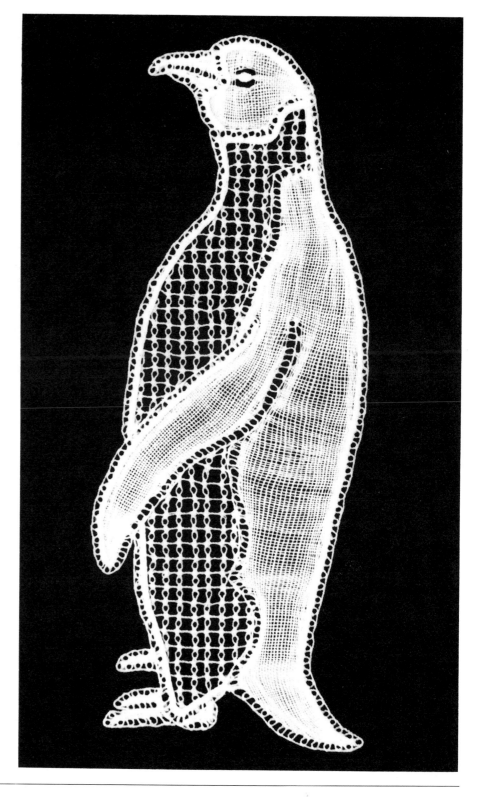

Fig. 23a right side

Am Auge die Rißpaare in drei Teile teilen, wobei für die Mitte zwei Paare vorzusehen sind. Mit den zwei mittleren Paaren ein Formschlag-Blatt, dann Kopf und Gesicht im Leinenschlag klöppeln, und die mittleren Paare am Ende des Auges wieder aufnehmen.

Deel bij het oog de hangende paren in drieën, houd twee paar voor het midden. Klos een blaadje met de twee middenparen, klos beide zijden van de kop in linnenslag en voeg ze weer samen aan de basis van het oog.

Partager les passives en 3 au niveau de l'oeil en laissant 2 paires pour travailler l'oeil en point d'esprit. Reprendre toutes les paires pour continuer la tête en toile.

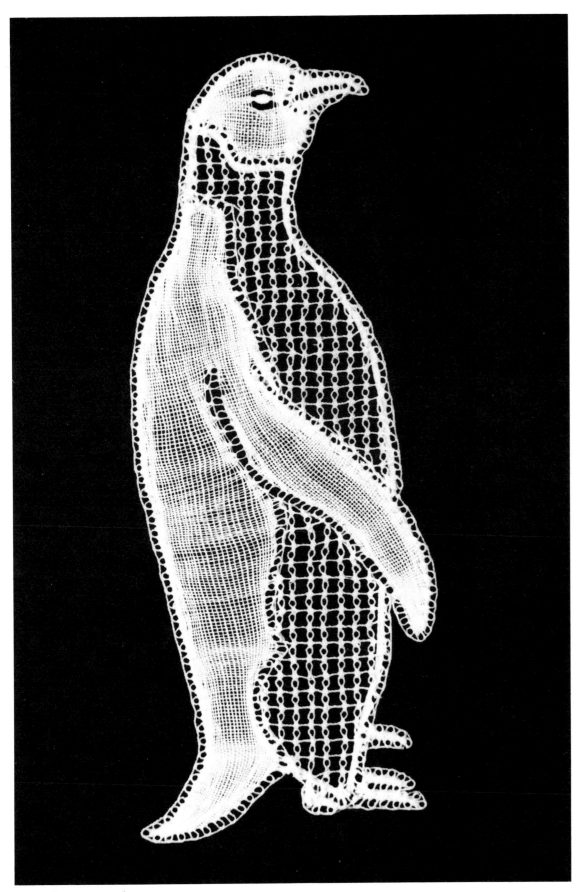

Fig. 23b wrong side

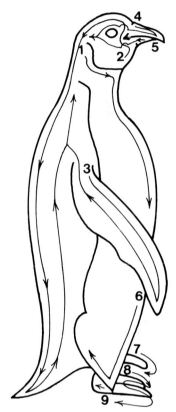

Fig. 23c   working order

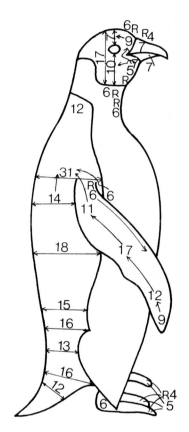

Fig. 23d   number of pairs

Filling: Pin and a Chain

Fig. 23e   pricking

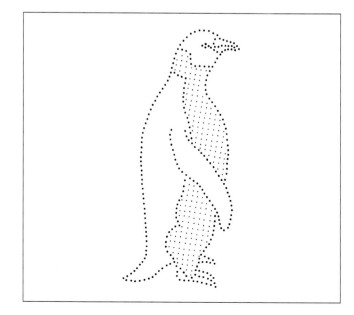

24 Dolphin

Make the fin (1) with 4 pairs of rib, and whole stitch. This will be covered by the body.

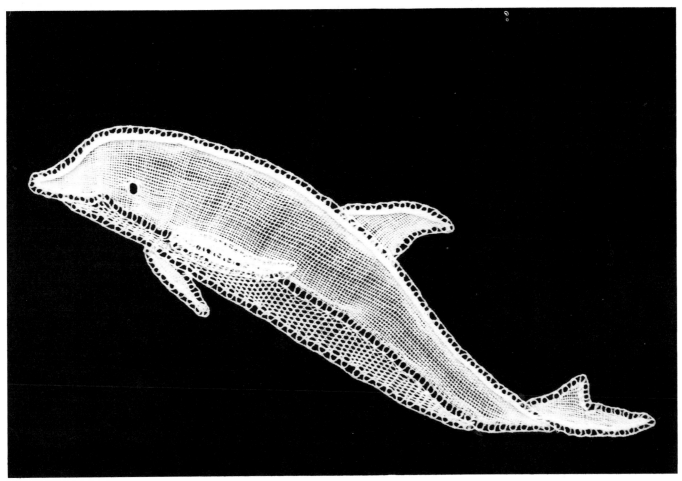

Fig. 24a   right side

Fig. 24c   working order

Die Flosse (1) mit einer Vier-Paar-Rippe und Leinenschlag klöppeln; sie wird vom Körper bedeckt.

Klos de vin (1) met 4-parige rib en linnenslag. Het lijf komt hier overheen.

Faire l'aileron (1) avec 4 paires en lacet contour et toile. Il sera recouvert par le corps.

Fig. 24b   wrong side

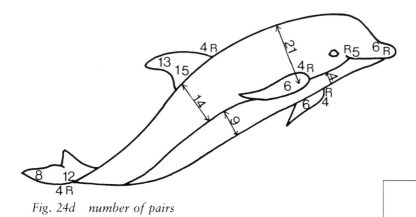

Fig. 24d   number of pairs

Fig. 24e   prickings

76

25 Puffin

Make the face with half stitch, take two pairs at the eye, make a triangle (start as leaf and finish as tally); cover with half stitch, join two pairs and continue.

Fig. 25a right side

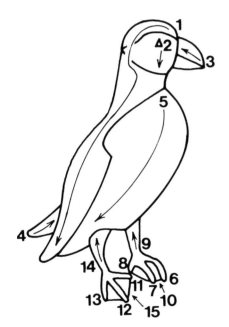

Fig. 25c working order

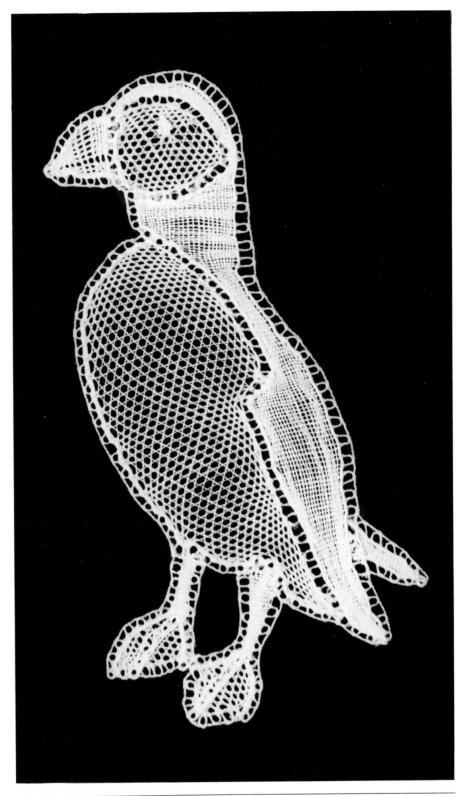

Das Gesicht mit Halbschlag ausführen; für die Augen zwei Paare verwenden, um ein Dreieck im Formschlag zu klöppeln (als Blatt beginnen und als Quadrat beenden); mit Halbschlag bedecken, zwei Paare hinzufügen und weiterklöppeln.

Klos de kop in netslag, neem bij het oog twee paar, maak hiermee een driehoek (begin als blaadje en eindig als moes); klos hierover in netslag, voeg de twee paar weer in en werk verder.

La tête en point simple. Prendre 2 paires pour l'oeil et faire un point d'esprit triangulaire. Superposer la grille et reprendre les paires de l'oeil en temps voulu en pt s., dans l'ordre initial.

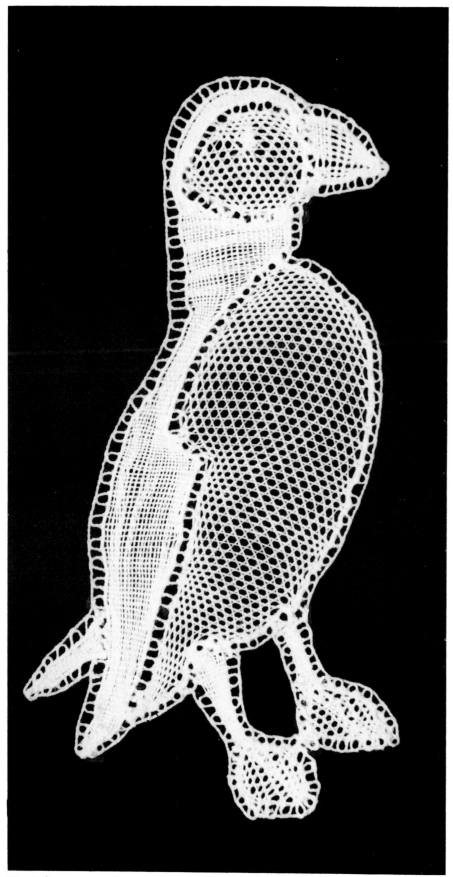

Fig. 25b   wrong side

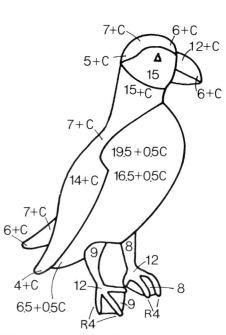

Fig. 25d   number of pairs

Fig. 25e   pricking

78

26   Teddy Bear

Cover the rib with half stitch until
you reach the base of the ear;
leave the threads to one side while
working whole stitch at the head;
join all the threads together and
work the remainder of the face
and behind the ear.

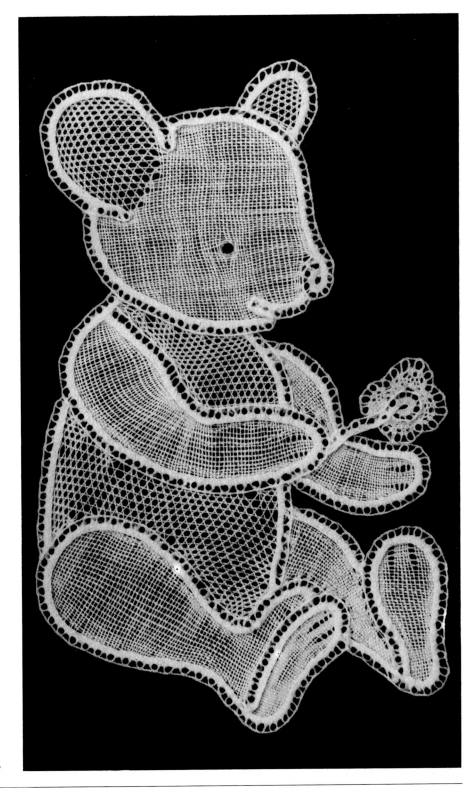

Fig. 26a   right side

Die Rippe mit Halbschlag bedecken, bis
man den unteren Teil des Ohrs erreicht;
die Fäden an einer Seite liegen lassen,
während man den Kopf im Leinenschlag
ausführt; alle Fäden vereinen und das
restliche Gesicht und die Partie unter dem
Ohr klöppeln.

Klos in netslag over de rib tot de basis
van het oor; leg de klossen opzij terwijl U
de kop in linnenslag klost; voeg alles
samen en klos de rest van het gezicht en
achter het oor.

Couvrir le lacet contour de l'oreille en
grille jusqu'à sa base. Laisser en attente.
Commencer alors la tête en toilé. Ajouter
peu à peu les paires en attente de l'oreille.
Continuer ainsi le toilé avec toutes les
paires et en ajouter derrière l'oreille.

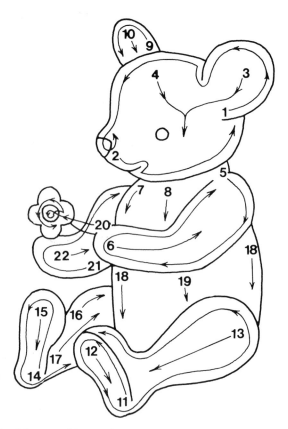

Fig. 26c   working order

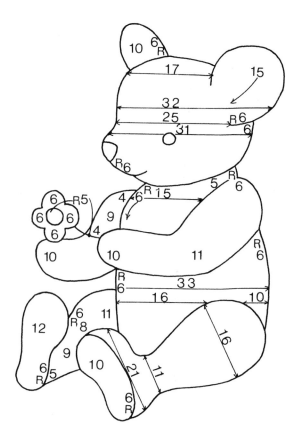

Fig. 26d   number of pairs

Fig. 26e   pricking

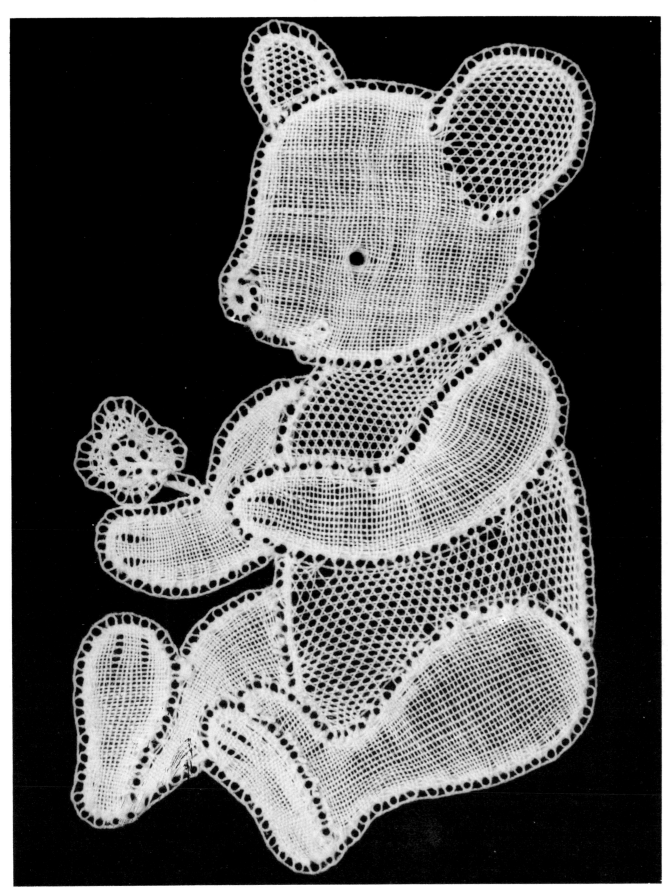

Fig. 26b   wrong side

27 Lovebird

Joining the neck and wing: sew six pairs into the beak; make a rib as far as the nearest pinhole to the wing; after the edge stitch twist the runner five times; sew into the wing, twist once, sew into the bar, twist again, make whole stitch with the edge pair and continue the rib.

Fig. 27a   right side

Um den Hals mit dem Flügel zu verbinden, werden sechs Paare am Schnabel eingehäkelt; eine Rippe bis zum nächsten Nadelpunkt klöppeln; nach dem Randschlag das Laufpaar fünfmal drehen; in den Flügel einhäkeln, einmal drehen, in das Band einhäkeln, nochmals drehen, mit dem Randpaar im Leinenschlag fortfahren und die Rippe weiterklöppeln.

Samenvoegen van nek en vleugel; hang zes paar in de snavel; klos een rib tot de dichtstbij de vleugel zijnde speld; draai het looppaar na de randslag vijf keer; haak aan in de vleugel, draai één keer, haak aan in het koordje, draai weer, klos linnenslag met het randpaar en ga verder met de rib.

Pour joindre le cou à l'aile accrocher 6 paires sur le bec. Faire un lacet contour jusqu'à l'aile, après le point de bordure faire 5 torsions sur les voyageurs, accrocher sur l'aile, 1 torsion, pt t. avec la passive de bordure et reprendre le lacet contour.

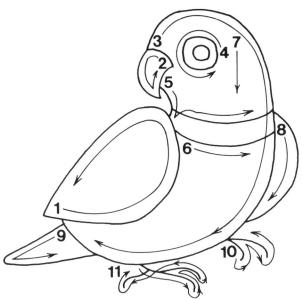

Fig. 27c   *working order*

Fig. 27b   *wrong side*

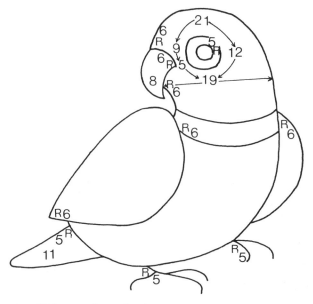

Fig. 27d   *number of pairs*

Fillings: Italian, Pin and a Stitch and Trolly Net

Fig. 27e   *pricking*

28 Alexander Parakeet

(Alexander has been a friend of mine for many years.) Twist the runners to make the windows in the wing and the tail.

Fig. 28a   right side

(Alexander war jahrelang mein Freund.) Das Durchbruchmuster in Flügel und Schwanz erhält man durch Drehen des Laufpaars.

(Alexander is vele jaren mijn vriend geweest.) Draai de lopers om de open luchtjes in de vleugel en de staart te maken.

Alexandre fut mon ami pendant des années. Torsions des voyageurs pour ajourer les ailes et la queue.

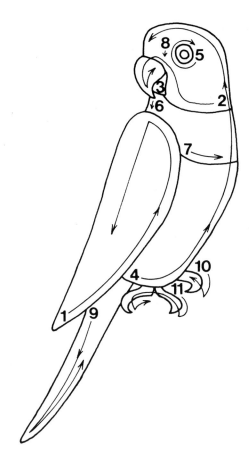

Fig. 28c   working order

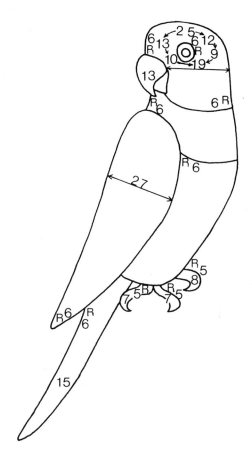

Fig. 28d   number of pairs

Filling: Italian *and* Pin and a Stitch

Fig. 28e   pricking

Fig. 28b   wrong side

29 Cat

Make the head in whole stitch; divide into three parts for the eyes. Make each eye with a leaf, re-joining them to continue the face. The nose is made with two central passive pairs worked as a triangular tally, twisting each pair seven times for the whiskers. Cover with whole stitch.

Fig. 29a right side

Den Kopf im Leinenschlag ausführen; für die Augen die Klöppel in drei Teile teilen. Das Auge mit einem Formschlag-Blättchen klöppeln, und das Gesicht mit allen Paaren weiterarbeiten. Die Nase besteht aus einem Formschlag-Dreieck, das mit den zwei mittleren Rißpaaren ausgeführt wird; jedes Paar siebenmal für die Schnurrhaare drehen. Mit Leinenschlag bedecken.

Klos de kop in linnenslag; verdeel in drieën door de ogen. Klos voor elk oog een blaadje, voeg weer samen voor de rest van het gezicht. Voor de neus zijn twee middelste hangende paren gewerkt als driehoekige vormslag, waarna elk paar zeven keer is gedraaid voor de snor. Klos hier overheen linnenslag.

Faire la tête en point toile. Partager en 3 pour les yeux. Faire chaque oeil avec un point d'esprit. Réintroduire les paires pour continuer la tête. Le nez se fait avec 2 paires centrales en point d'esprit triangulaire. Tordre chaque paire 7 fois pour les moustaches. Couvrir avec le point toile.

Fig. 29b   *wrong side*

Fig. 29c   *working order*

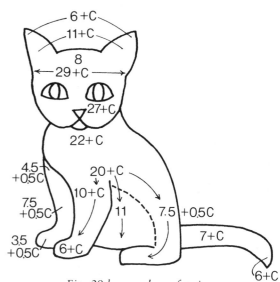

Fig. 29d   *number of pairs*

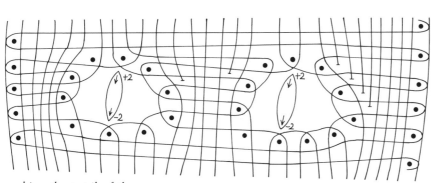

making the pupil of the eye

Fig. 29e   *pricking*

88

30 Kitten

Start at the tops of the ears, make the face and chest. Leave all the threads without sewing. Make the outline of the boot. Sew all the threads at the outline of the boot (no. 8, diag. 30c).

Fig. 30a   right side

An den Ohrenspitzen beginnen, das Gesicht und die Brust klöppeln. Alle Fäden ohne Einhäkeln liegen lassen. Die Stiefelumrandung klöppeln, und alle Fäden in die Stiefelumrandung einhäkeln (Punkt 8, Abb. *30-c*).

Begin aan de punt van de oren, klos kop en lijf. Laat alle klossen liggen zonder aan te haken. Klos de omtrek van de laars. Haak alle paren aan in de omtrek van de laars. (nr 8, diag. 30c).

Commencer en haut des oreilles. Faire la tête et le poitrail. Laisser en attente les fuseaux. Faire le contour du chausson. Accrocher alors les fuseaux en attente sur ce lacet contour. (8 diag. 30c).

Fig. 30b   wrong side

Fig. 30c   *working order*

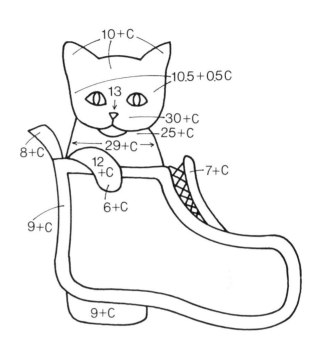

Fig. 30d   *number of pairs*

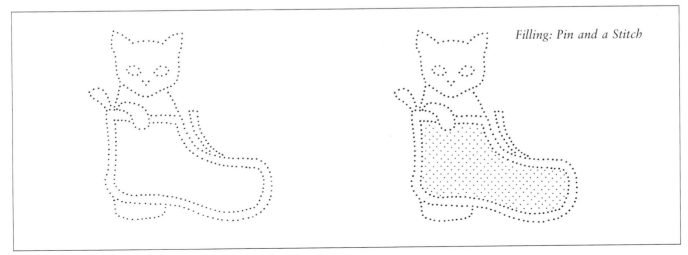

Filling: Pin and a Stitch

Fig. 30e   *prickings*

31 Welsh Corgi

Start at the base of the ear with rib; change to half stitch, and work towards the chest.

Fig. 31a   right side

Unten am Ohr mit einer Rippe beginnen, zu Halbschlag übergehen und zur Brust hin klöppeln.

Begin aan de basis van het oor met een rib; ga over in netslag en klos naar de borst.

Commencer à la base de l'oreille par un lacet contour, changer en grille et descendre le poitrail.

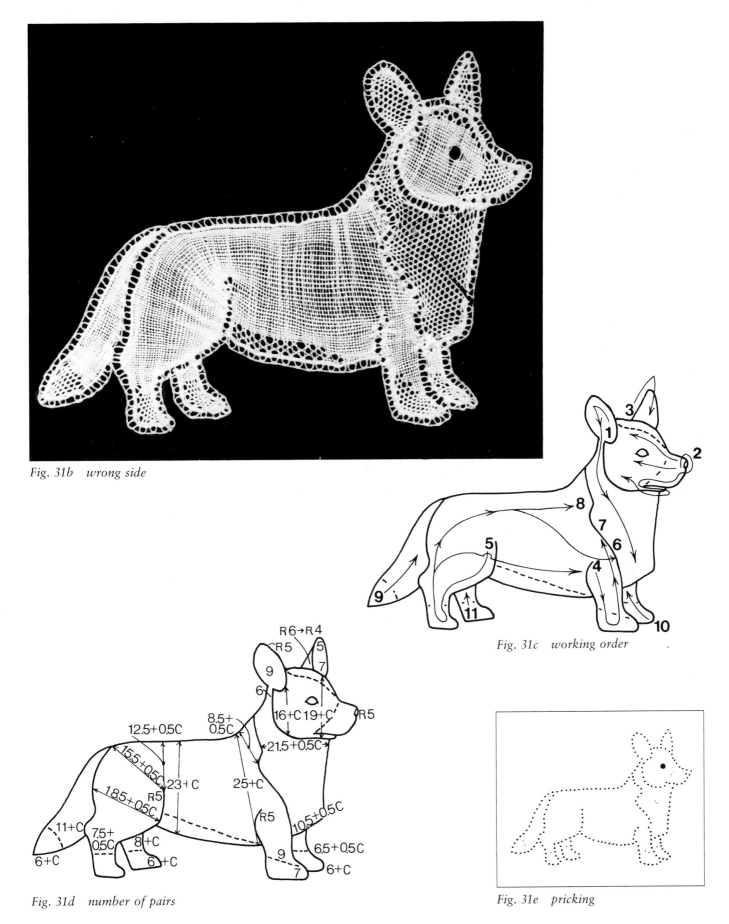

Fig. 31b   wrong side

Fig. 31c   working order

Fig. 31d   number of pairs

Fig. 31e   pricking

32 Hare

Make the outline of the face in rib; weave in a coarse pair at the base of the ear, make the outside of the ear, and then the inside, crossing the passives from the face and ear.

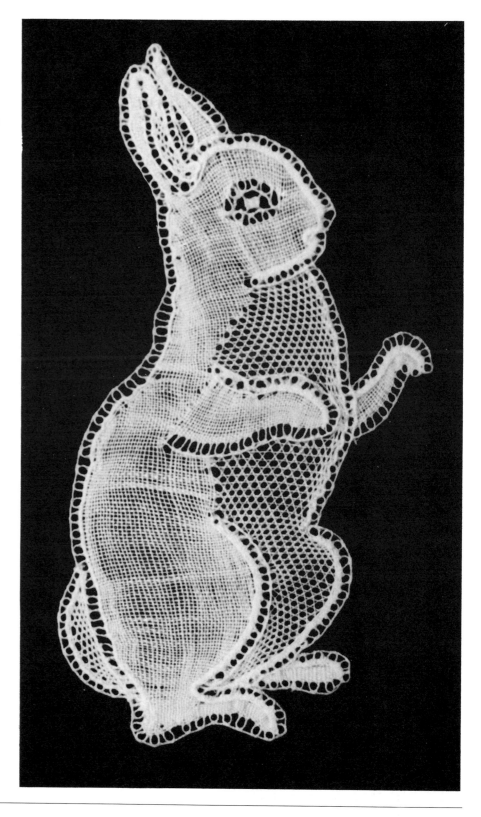

Fig. 32a   right side

Das Gesicht mit einer Rippe umranden; ein Paar mit dickem Garn unten am Ohr einklöppeln, die Innenseite, dann die Außenseite des Ohrs ausführen, wobei die Rißpaare von Gesicht und Ohr gekreuzt werden.

Klos een rib voor de omtrek van het gezicht; weef een dik paar in aan de onderkant van het oor, klos de buitenkant van het oor en dan de binnenkant, werk de hangende paren van gezicht en oor dooreen.

Commencer en lacet contour par la tête. Ajouter le gros fil à la base de l'oreille. Faire l'extérieur puis l'intérieur de l'oreille. Croiser les passives de la tête et de l'oreille.

94

Fig. 32b wrong side

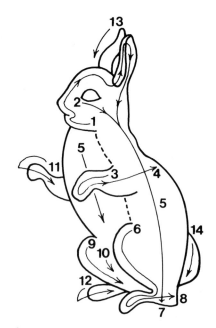

Fig. 32c   working order

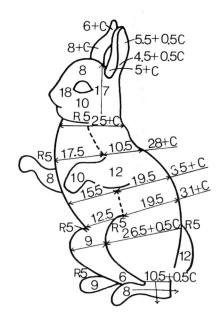

Fig. 32d   number of pairs

Fig. 32e   pricking

33 Goldfish (2)

This pattern is designed for flat Honiton, but you can change it for raised Honiton for the four fins and tail.

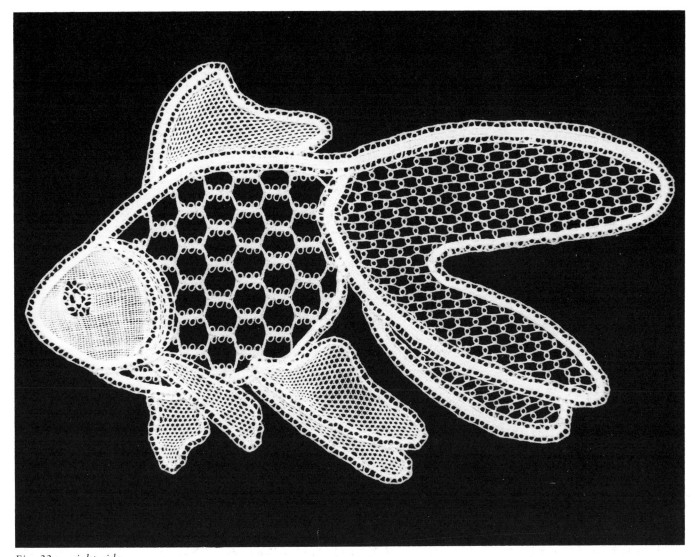

Fig. 33a *right side*

Dieses Motiv ist als flache Honiton-Spitze entworfen; Flossen und Schwanz können jedoch auch erhaben ausgeführt werden.

Dit patroon is ontworpen voor vlakke Honiton, U kunt de vier vinnen en de staart ook in 'raised Honiton' klossen.

C'est un modèle 'Honiton' plat qui peut être interprété en bords reliefs pour la queue et les nageoires.

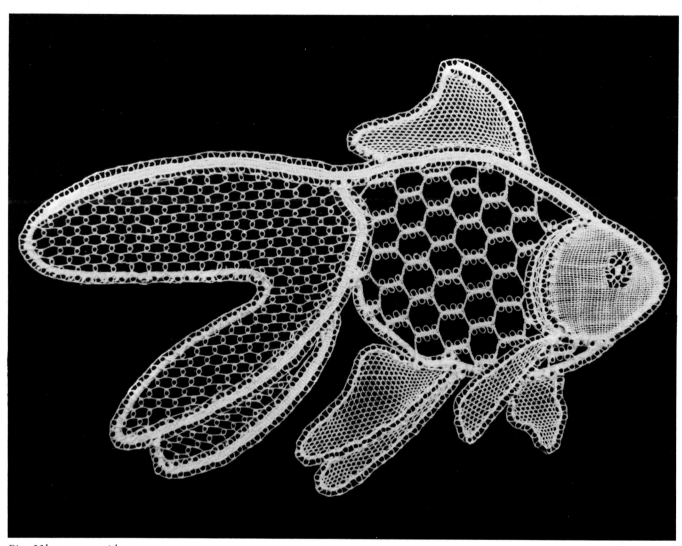

Fig. 33b   wrong side

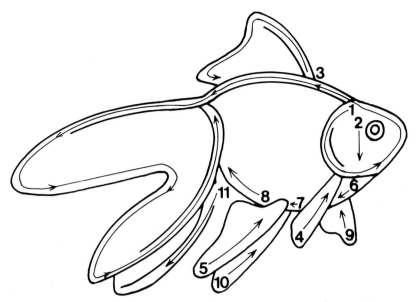

Fig. 33c   *working order*

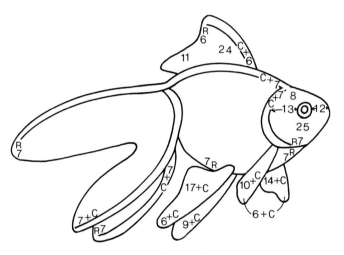

Fig. 33d   *number of pairs*

Filling: Whole Stitch Block and Pin and a Stitch

Fig. 33e   *prickings*

34 Sparrow

This Japanese sparrow pattern is inspired by a lovely old story, in which the sparrow gives good luck to an old man who saved her life.

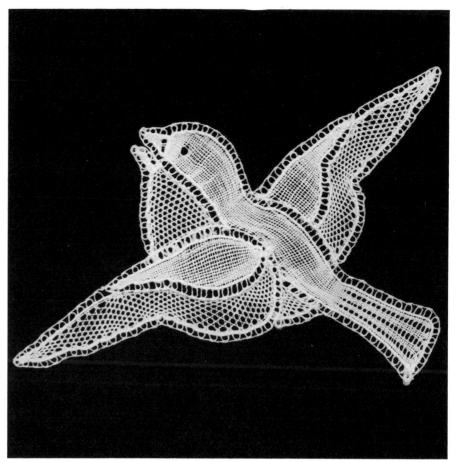

Fig. 34a   right side

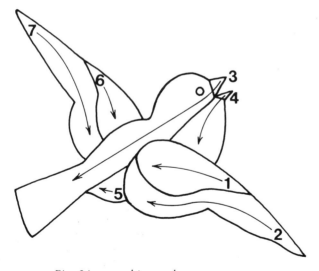

Fig. 34c   working order

Diese Wiedergabe eines japanischen Spatzes erinnert an eine schöne alte Geschichte, in der ein Spatz einem alten Mann, der ihm das Leben gerettet hatte, Glück bringt.

Deze Japanse mus is geinspireerd op een leuk oud verhaal, waarin de mus geluk brengt aan een oude man die haar leven heeft gered.

Ce moineau Japonais nous vient d'un vieux conte où le moineau porte chance à un vieil homme qui lui avait sauvé la vie.

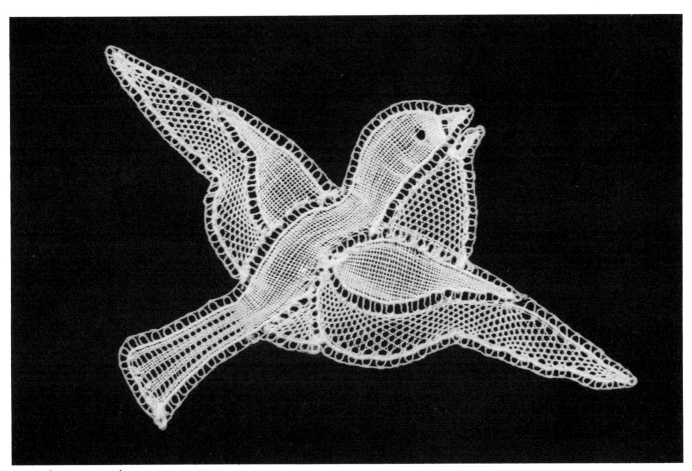

Fig. 34b   wrong side

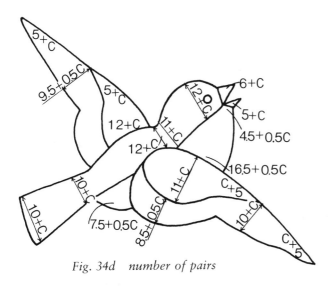

5+C

9.5+0.5C

5+C

12+C

12+C

10+C

10+C

7.5+0.5C

8.5+0.5C

11+C

11+C

12+C

6+C

5+C

4.5+0.5C

16.5+0.5C

C+5

10+C

C+5

Fig. 34d   number of pairs

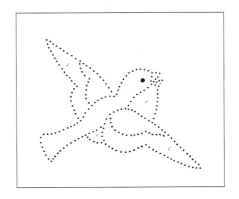

Fig. 34e   pricking

35 Wild Goose

Make the eye with five pairs of rib; cover with whole stitch, setting up a thicker pin in the centre of the eye.

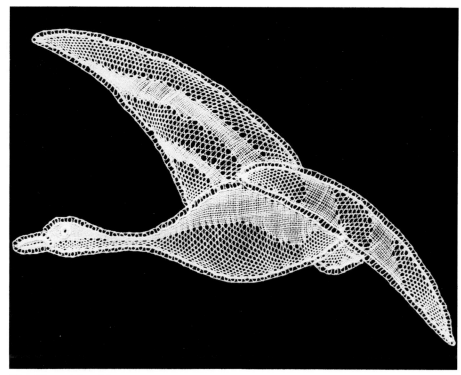

Fig. 35a   right side

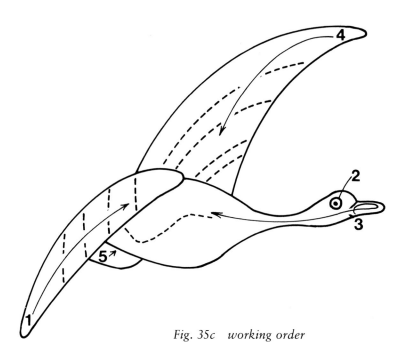

Fig. 35c   working order

Das Auge mit fünf Paaren der Rippe ausführen; mit Leinenschlag bedecken, wobei eine dicke Nadel in die Augenmitte gesteckt wird.

Klos het oog als 5-parige rib; klos hier over in linnenslag, waarbij U midden in het oog een dikke speld zet.

Faire l'oeil en lacet contour avec 5 paires. Recouvrir de toilé en plaçant une plus grosse épingle pour marquer le centre de l'oeil.

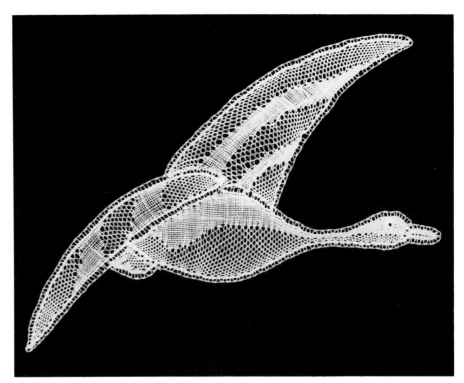

Fig. 35b   wrong side

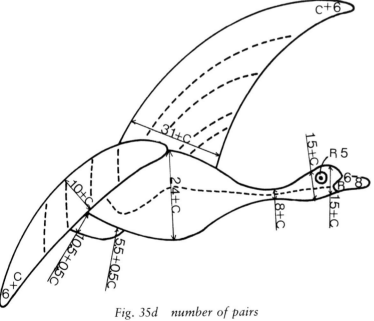

Fig. 35d   number of pairs

Fig. 35e   pricking

36 Female Mandarin Duck

A pair of mandarin ducks is a frequently used motif at silver and gold wedding anniversaries, and other celebrations.

Fig. 36a   right side

Ein Mandarin-Enten-Pärchen wird häufig als Symbol bei Silber-und Gold-Hochzeiten und anderen Festen dargestellt.

Regelmatig wordt een paar Mandarijneenden gebruikt als motief bij Zilveren of Gouden bruiloft en andere feesten.

On voit souvent un motif de couple de Duc Mandarin pour des noces d'or ou d'argent ou autres festivités.

Fig. 36b   wrong side

Fig. 36c   working order

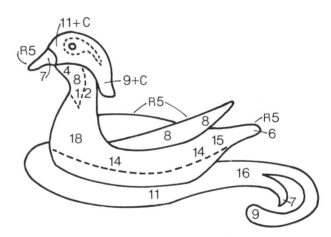

Fig. 36d   number of pairs

Fig. 36e   pricking

37 Male Mandarin Duck

Make six pairs of rib (3); work half stitch at the base of the wing. Roll up six pairs, hang 17 pairs in the pinholes, and make the wing in whole stitch. Make the first toe with five pairs, leave this and make the remaining toes. Re-join them to make the leg and finally the webbed foot.

Fig. 37a   right side

Eine Sechs-Paar-Rippe klöppeln (3); am Beginn des Flügels einen Halbschlag klöppeln. Eine Rolle mit sechs Paaren bilden, 17 Paare an eine Nadel hängen und den Flügel im Leinenschlag ausführen. Die erste Zehe mit fünf Paaren klöppeln, die Paare liegen lassen, und die übrigen Zehen ausführen. Mit allen Paaren den Fuß und abschließend die Schwimmhaut zwischen den Zehen klöppeln.

Klos een 6-parige rib (3); klos netslag aan de aanzet van de vleugel. Rol met zes paar terug, hang 17 paar in de speldegaatjes, en klos de vleugel in linnenslag. Klos de eerste teen met vijf paar, leg ze opzij en klos de overige tenen. Voeg ze samen voor de poot en klos tot slot de zwemvliezen.

Prendre 6 paires pour le lacet contour. A la base de l'aile faire en point simple. Ramener en fagot tordu, ajouter 17 paires sur les trous d'épingle et faire l'aile en toile. Faire le premier doigt avec 5 paires, laisser en attente. Faire les suivants et regrouper tous les fuseaux pour faire la patte. Finir la palme.

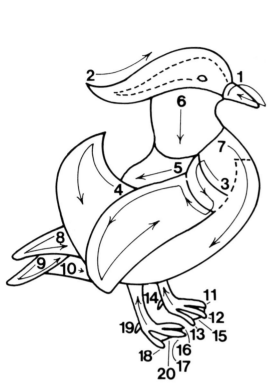

Fig. 37c *working order*

Fig. 37b *wrong side*

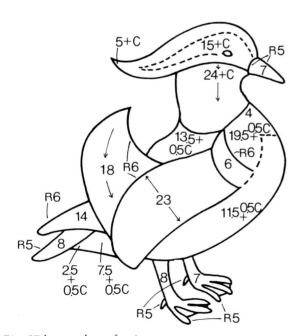

Fig. 37d *number of pairs*

Fig. 37e *pricking*

38 Crane

When making the wing, weave the coarse thread at the divide, twist all the passive threads, and work back the coarse thread. The crane symbolizes long life, and this motif is used at weddings, special birthdays, and other celebrations.

Fig. 38a right side

Beim Fügel den dicken Faden an der Teilung einweben, alle Rißpaare drehen, und mit dem dicken Faden zurückklöppeln. Der Kranich symbolisiert langes Leben und erscheint als Motiv bei Hochzeiten, Geburtstagen und anderen Anlässen.

Weef bij het klossen van de vleugel de dikke draad op de splitsing door de hangende paren, draai deze paren en werk de dikke draad weer terug. De Kraanvogel is het symbool voor een lang leven. Dit motief wordt gebruikt bij huwelijken, bizondere verjaardagen en andere feesten.

Une grue est symbole de longue vie. Ce modèle est donc utilisé pour les mariages, naissance ou autre fête.

Fig. 38b   wrong side

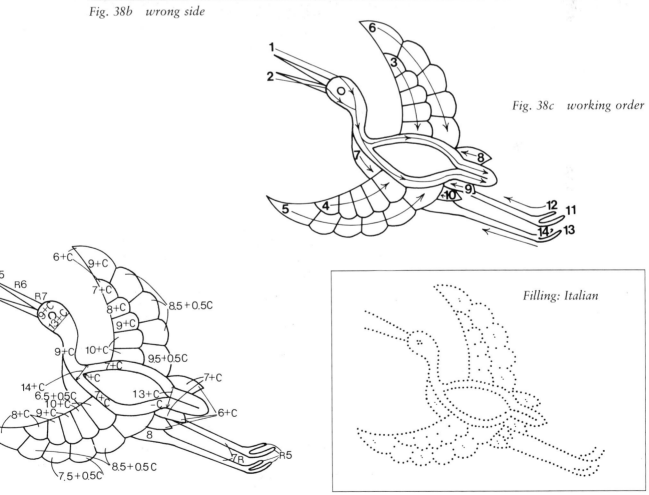

Fig. 38c   working order

Fig. 38d   number of pairs

Fig. 38e   pricking

Filling: Italian

109

39 Turtle

This filling was created especially for this pattern. The turtle symbolizes long life and is often used decoratively with a crane.

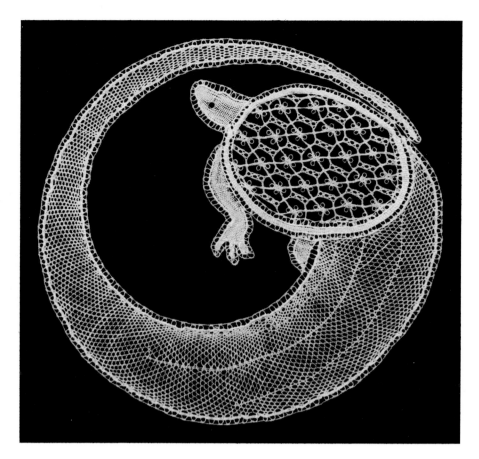

Fig. 39a   right side

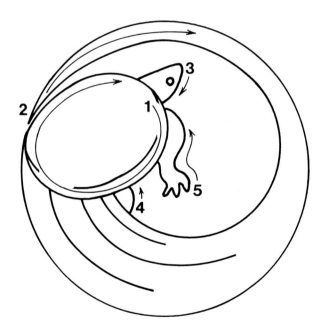

Fig. 39c   working order

Der Füllgrund wurde speziell für dieses Motiv geschaffen. Die Schildkröte gilt als Symbol für ein langes Leben und wird als Dekor häufig zusammen mit einem Kranich gezeigt.

Deze vulling is speciaal voor dit patroon ontworpen. De Schildpad symboliseert een lang leven en wordt decoratief vaak samen met de Kraanvogel gebruikt.

La tortue aussi symbolise la longue vie et est souvent associée à la grue.

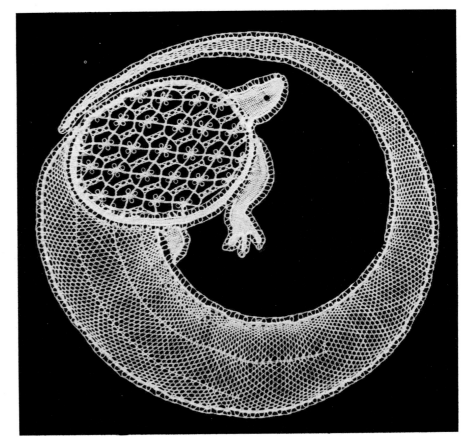

Fig. 39b   wrong side

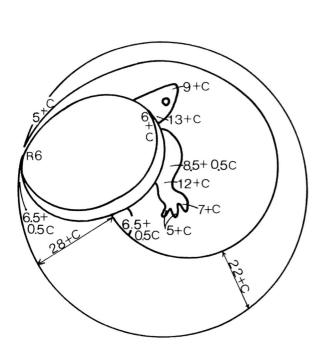

Fig. 39d   number of pairs

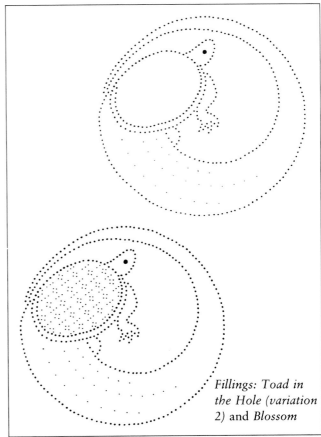

Fillings: Toad in
the Hole (variation
2) and Blossom

Fig. 39e   prickings

40 Phoenix

It is said in Japan that a phoenix
will appear in public to herald the
birth of a great emperor.

Fig. 40a   right side

In Japan wird behauptet, daß ein Phönix
sich dem Volke zeigen wird, um die
Geburt eines großen Kaisers anzukündigen.

In Japan wordt gezegd dat er een Feniks
zal verschijnen om de geboorte van een
groot keizer aan te kondigen.

On dit au Japon qu'un phoenix
apparaîtra pour annoncer la venue au
monde d'un grand empereur.

Fig. 40b   wrong side

Fig. 40c   working order

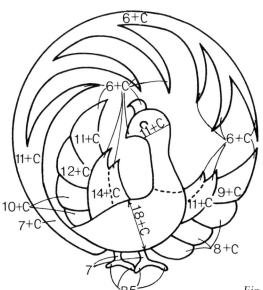

Fig. 40d   number of pairs

Fig. 40e   pricking

Appendix 1: Fillings

The great variety of fillings is one of the characteristic features of Honiton lace. Many Honiton lacemakers prick their fillings by eye, without the aid of graph paper, sometimes using a ruler as a guide. This makes it possible to fit a filling into a given shape in such a way that the groups of holes are complete at the edges and matching at both sides. An example of such filling worked into a curved space can be seen in Pattern 21. However, to give the student some idea of the size the fillings should be, grid prickings are shown on p. 127. Fillings should be pricked on *one millimetre graph paper*.

The pairs for the fillings are sewn into the completed braid above and as near as possible to the groups of holes where they will be required, and often more than one pair will need to be sewn into the same hole. When sewing out pairs which have worked a row of filling, they are either tied three times and laid back to be cut off later, or they are brought in again to be used in a subsequent row if they are needed to fill in a widening space.

When a filling has been completed, and all the pairs have been sewn out and tied, the bobbins must be cut off and the ends of the thread trimmed before the pins are removed from the filling. Take out all the pins from the filling.

It often happens that the groups of holes of which many fillings consist are not complete at the edges of the space to be filled. When this happens, work the incomplete group as nearly as possible to the instructions given for these fillings – it is often possible to make a sewing into the edge of the braid to replace any missing holes.

1. Füllungen kann man mit Hilfe eines Lineals oder nach Augenmaß vorstechen. So ist es möglich, komplette Gruppen von Löchern unregelmäßigen Formen einzupassen (z.B. Muster 21).
2. Werden Gitter benutzt, sticht man auf 1 mm-Papier.
3. Bei den Füllungen werden je nach Bedarf ein oder mehr Paare (P) in die geklöppelten Bänder so dicht wie möglich an den Lochgruppierungen angehäkelt.
4. Paare für eine Anzahl von Füllungen werden in das Bändchen eingehäkelt, 3 x geknotet, später abgeschnitten oder für die nächste Füllung benutzt.
5. Ist die Füllung beendet, abhäkeln und die übrigen Fäden 3 x knoten. Fäden kurz abschneiden, Nadeln entfernen.
6. Wird ein vorgestochenes Gitter benutzt, kann es vorkommen, daß Lochgruppierungen unvollständig sind. Soweit wie möglich arbeiten, in die Bändchen einhäkeln, um ein evtl. fehlendes Loch zu ersetzen.

1. Vullingen kunnen met behulp van een lineaal worden geprikt of 'op het oog', zodat complete groepen van gaatjes in onregelmatige vormen gepast kunnen worden (bv. zie Patroon 21).
2. Prik, als U 'grids' gebruikt, op 1 mm ruitjespapier.
3. hang voor vullingen het gewenste aantal paren (pr of prn) zo dicht mogelijk bij de gaatjesgroepjes in aan voltooide bandjes.
4. Paren die voor rijen vullingen gebruikt zijn, worden in een bandje aangehaakt, dan 3 maal geknoopt om later te worden afgeknipt, of opnieuw gebruikt, voor de volgende rij van de vulling.
5. Haak, als een vulling klaar is, aan en knoop alle overblijvende paren 3 maal.

Knip de draden netjes bij en verwijder daarna de spelden uit de vulling.
6. Bij gebruik van een geprikte 'grid', kan het voorkomen dat een groepje gaatjes niet compleet is. Klos dan zoveel mogelijk en haak aan in een bandje als U een gaatje moet vervangen.

1. Le piquage des fonds peut être fait à l'aide d'une règle ou à main levée; ceci permet de loger des groupes entiers de trous dans des formes irrégulières (*voir* par exemple l'ouvrage 21).
2. Si vous utilisez un gabarit, faites le piquage sur du papier millimétrique.
3. Pour les fonds, crochetez une ou plusieurs paires (prs), autant que nécessaire, dans les lacets terminés, aussi près que possible des groupes de trous.
4. Les prs utilisées pour finir sont crochetées dans le lacet, puis nouées 3 fois pour être coupées ensuite ou réutilisées pour la rangée suivante du fond.
5. Une fois le fond terminé, crochetez et nouez 3 fois toutes les prs restantes. Coupez les fils, puis enlevez les épingles du fond.
6. Si vous utilisez un gabarit perforé, certains groupes de trous peuvent être incomplets. Travaillez le plus loin possible en crochetant dans le lacet si vous devez mettre en place un trou supplémentaire.

How to prick

Transfer the dots for the chosen filling onto tracing paper, lay this over the pricking, and prick through into the space to be filled. Another method is to prick a block of the filling onto a piece of acetate, or a used and washed X-ray plate; this is laid over the pricking and pricked through onto the pattern. These pricked 'templates' can be used again and again, providing that the pricking is done carefully, so as not to enlarge the holes in the template.

Das Stechen

1. Das gewünschte Pricking nachzeichnen, auf das Muster legen und auf die zu füllende Fläche stechen

oder

2. Die gewünschte Fläche des Pricking auf transparenten Film stechen. Als Schablone benutzen und vorsichtig auf das Muster stechen, damit man die Schablone mehrmals verwenden kann.

Hoe te prikken

1. Neem de gekozen 'gridpricking' over, leg die op het patroon en prik hem door in de te vullen ruimte.
2. Prik een gedeelte van 'grid pricking'

over op een vel stevig doorzichtig plastic. Gebruik dit als model en prik dan zorgvuldig (zodat het model vaker kan worden gebruikt) op het patroon.

Piquage

1. Tracez le gabarit choisi, posez-le sur le dessin et perforez l'espace à remplir.
2. Perforez une surface du gabarit sur un film transparent. Utilisez-le comme modèle et perforez le carton soigneusement (afin de pouvoir le réutiliser).

Abbreviations

pr(s)   pair(s)
WS   whole stitch
TW(S)   twist(s)
plt(s)   plait(s)
HS   half stitch

Abkürzungen

dr.   drehen
FL   Flechter

GZS   Ganzschlag (kr., dr., kr., dr.)
kr.   kreuzen
LS   Leinenschlag (Kr., dr., kr.)
N.   Nadel
P.   Paar(e)
wdh.   wiederholen

Afkortingen

pr(n)   paar(paren)
lsl   linnenslag
dr(n)   draai(-en)
vl(n)   vlecht(-en)
nsl   netslag

Abreviations des termes techniques

ép.   épingle
p.   paire
pt t.   point toile ou toilé
pt dble   point double
t.   torsion
C4   corde de 4
pt s.   point simple ou grille
gche   gauche
dte   droite

Whole Stitch Block

1. Sew in 4 prs above each block, preferably 2 prs to left of left pin, and 2 prs to right of right pin. TW each pr once.

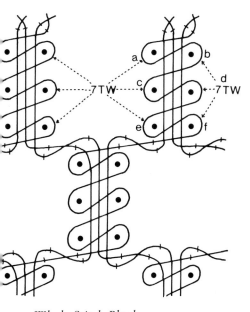

Whole Stitch Block

2. To work one block, take right pr in WS through 3 prs to left, TW 7 times, and put up pin *a*.
3. Take runners, WS to right through 3 prs, TW 7 times, and put up pin *b*.
4. Repeat **2** and **3** for pins *c, d, e,* and *f*.
5. Take runners from *f* to left through 3 prs in WS.
6. Work WS with 2 passive prs on right.
7. TW each pr once.
8. Work WS, TW with left 2 prs.
9. Work WS, TW with right 2 prs.
10. Complete each block working **2–9**, with 2 prs from the right and 2 prs from the left.

1. Über jedem Block 4 P. einhäkeln, u.z. vorzugsweise 2 P. links von der linken N. und 2 P. rechts von der rechten N. Jedes P. 1x dr.
2. Für einen Block läuft das rechte P. im LS durch 3 linke P., 7x dr., N. in *a* stechen.

3. Mit Laufp. im LS nach rechts durch 3 P. klöppeln, 7x dr., N. in *b* stechen.
4. Punkte 2 und 3 bei N. *c, d, e* und *f* wdh.
5. Mit Laufp. von *f* nach links durch 3 P. im LS klöppeln.
6. Rechts im LS durch 2 Rißp. klöppeln.
7. Jedes P. 1x dr.
8. LS, die 2 linken P. dr.
9. LS, die 2 rechten P. dr.
10. Jeden Block von Punkt 2–9 mit je 2 P. von rechts und links ausführen.

1. Hang boven ieder blok 4 pr in, liefst 2 pr links van linker speld, en 2 pr rechts van rechter speld. Dr elk pr 1 keer.
2. Voor één blok, met rechter pr in lsl door 3 pr naar links, dr 7 keer, en zet speld *a*.
3. Met lopers in lsl naar rechts door 3 pr, dr 7 keer, en zet speld b.
4. Herhaal **2** en **3** voor spelden *c, d, e* en *f*.
5. Met lopers in lsl van *f* naar links door 3 pr.
6. Lsl met 2 rechter hangende prn.
7. Dr elk pr 1 keer.
8. Met 2 linker prn lsl, dr.

9. Met 2 rechter prn lsl, dr.
10. Klos elk blok volgens **2–9**, met 2 pr van rechts en 2 pr van links.

1. Accrocher 4 p. au-dessus de chaque pavé, de préférence 2 p. à gauche de l'ép. gche et 2 p. à dte de l'ép. dte; 1 t. sur chaque p.
2. Avec la p. de dte traverser en pt t. 3 p. vers la gche, 7 t., ép. sur a.
3. Les voyageurs vont à dte en pt t., 7 t., ép. sur b.
4. Répéter 2 et 3 pour les ép. c, d, e, f.
5. Les voyageurs de f reviennent sur 3 p. en pt t.
6. Pt t. avec les 2 passives du pavé à dte.
7. 1 t. sur chaque p.
8. Pt dble avec les 2 p. de gche du pavé.
9. Pt dble avec les 2 p. de dte du pavé.
10. Travailler chaque pavé de 2 à 9 en prenant 2 p. à dte et 2 p. à gche.

Whole Stitch Block Variation

Worked in the same way as 'Toad in the Hole (variation 1)', but omitting the square tallies.
1. Following the detail diagram, work **1–7** of variation 1.
2. Complete the block with two plts, one to the left and one to the right.

Wie bei 'Toad in the Hole'-Grund (Variante 1) vorgehen, jedoch die Formschlag-Quadrate weglassen.

1. Nach Detailzeichnung von Punkt *1–7* der oben genannten Variante *1* klöppeln.
2. Die Blocks mit 2 FL vervollständigen, davon einen FL nach links und einen FL nachs rechts arbeiten.

Wordt op dezelfde manier gewerkt als 'Toad in the Hole (variatie 1)', maar zonder de moezen.
1. Volg het detail diagram en klos **1–7** van variatie 1.
2. Maak het blok af met twee vln, één naar links en één naar rechts.

Voir 'Toad in the Hole (variation 1). Il n'y a pas de point d'esprit carré.
1. Suivre les explications 1 à 7 de la variation 1, voir détail sur diagramme.
2. Finir chaque pavé par 2 C4, une à gauche, une à droite.

Blossom

1. Sew in 2 prs at A, plt to first group of pinholes.
2. Sew in 2 prs at B, plt to first group of pinholes.
3. Use right pr from A to make a picot (7 TWS) on right at C, cover with WS, TW.
4. With centre 2 prs work WS TW.
5. With right 2 prs, WS, work a picot (7 TWS) on right at D, cover with WS, TW left pr once.
6. With left 2 prs, WS, work a picot (7 TWS) on left at E, cover with WS, TW right pr once.
7. With centre 2 prs work WS.
8. With right 2 prs, WS, work picot (7 TWS) on left at F.
9. Use each group of 2 prs to plt to next 2 groups of pinholes.

1. Bei A 2 P. einhäkeln, FL bis erste Lochgruppe klöppeln.
2. Bei B 2 P. einhäkeln, FL bis erste Lochgruppe klöppeln.
3. Mit dem rechten P. bei A einen Picot (7x dr.) rechts bei C machen, mit einem LS schließen, dr.
4. Mit den mittleren 2 P. einen GZS klöppeln.
5. Mit den rechten 2 P. einen LS, einen Picot (7x dr.) rechts bei D ausführen, mit einem LS schließen, links P. 1x dr.
6. Mit dem rechten P. einen LS, einen Picot (7x dr.) links bei E ausführen, mit einem LS schließen, rechtes P. 1x dr.
7. LS mit den 2 mittleren P.
8. Mit den 2 rechten P. GZS und einen Picot (7x dr.) links bei F machen.
9. Mit jeder Gruppe von 2 P. FL bis zu den nächsten 2 Lochgruppen klöppeln.

1. Hang 2 pr in bij A, vl tot eerste groep spelden.
2. Hang 2 pr in bij B, vl tot eerste groep spelden.
3. Maak rechts bij C een picot (7x dr) met rechter pr van A, sluit met lsl, dr.
4. Met 2 middenprn lsl dr.
5. Met 2 rechterprn lsl, maak rechts bij D, een picot (7x dr), sluit met lsl, dr linker pr 1x.
6. Met 2 linkerprn lsl, maak links bij E, een picot (7x dr), sluit met lsl, dr rechter pr 1x.
7. Met 2 middenprn lsl.
8. Met de 2 rechter prn lsl, maak een picot (7x dr) links, bij F.
9. Maak met iedere groep van 2 pr een vl naar de volgende 2 groepen spelden.

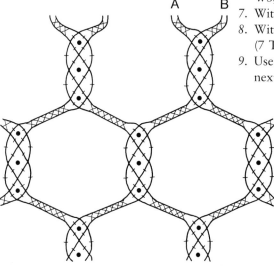

Whole Stitch Block (variation)

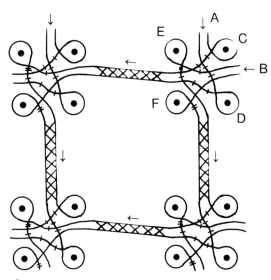

Blossom

1. Accrocher 2 p. sur *A* = C4 jusqu'au premier groupe d'ép.
2. Accrocher 2 p. sur *B* = C4 jusqu'au premier groupe d'ép.
3. Avec la p. à dte de *A* faire à dte sur *C* un picot tourné (7t) fermer l'ép. en pt dble.
4. Avec 2 p. centre = pt dble.
5. Avec 2 p. dte = pt t., picot tourné (7t.) à dte sur *D*, fermer l'ép. en pt t., 1 t. sur p. gche.
6. Avec 2 p. gche = pt t., picot tourné (7t.) à gche sur *E*, fermer l'ép. en pt t., 1 t. sur p. dte.
7. 2 p. centre = pt t.
8. 2 p. droite, pt t. = picot tourné (7t.) à gche sur *F*.
9. Prendre chaque groupe de 2p. Descendre en C4 jusqu'au prochain groupe d'ép.

Toad in the Hole

1. Each WS block is worked in the same way as for 'Whole Stitch Block' for pins *a–f*.
2. An additional 2 prs are sewn in above each block, TW each pr 5 times.
3. Each pr travels diagonally to the spaces between WS blocks, and 2 prs work a small square tally. TW each pr 5 times.
4. Each pr from a tally works diagonally in WS through 2 prs from a WS block to work another tally.

1. Jeder LS-Block wird bei N. *a–f* wie beim 'Whole Stitch Block'-Grund ausgeführt.
2. Über jedem Block werden 2 zusätzliche P. eingehäkelt; jedes P. 5x dr.
3. Jedes P. läuft schräg zur Lochmitte zwischen 2 LS-Blocks hin, die 2 P. treffen sich und bilden ein kleines Formschlag-Quadrat. Jedes P. 5x dr.
4. Jedes P. des Formschlag-Quadrats läuft schräg im LS durch 2 P. eines LS-Blocks, um ein weiteres Formschlag-Quadrat zu bilden.

1. Elk lsl-blok wordt voor de spelden *a–f* op dezelfde manier geklost als 'Whole Stitch Block'.
2. Hang boven blok 2 extra prn in, dr elk pr 5 keer.
3. Elk pr gaat diagonaal door de ruimte tussen de lsl-blokken, en 2 prn maken een kleine moes. Dr elk pr 5 keer.
4. Ieder pr van een moes gaat diagonaal in lsl door 2 pr van een lsl-blok om een nieuwe moes te maken.

1. Chaque pavé toilé suit la méthode 'Whole stitch block' pour les ép. de *a* à *f*.
2. Ajouter 2 p. au-dessus de chaque pavé. 5 t. sur chaque p.
3. Chaque p. suit une diagonale dans l'espace entre 2 pavés et elles se rencontrent en p. d'esprit carré. 5 t. sur chaque p. ensuite.
4. Chaque p. issue d'un pt d'esprit coupe en pt t. Les 2 p. issues du pavé toilé.

Toad in the Hole (variation 1)

In this variation the six-pin WS block is replaced with three pins, which are worked as follows (*see* detail diagram):
1. Sew in 2 prs at *A*, plt to first pin of block.
2. Sew in 2 prs at *B*, plt to first pin of block.
3. With centre 2 prs work WS TW, pin between them.
4. With left 2 prs, work WS TW, no pin.
5. With right 2 prs, work WS TW, no pin.
6. Repeat (**3, 4,** and **5**) × 2.
7. Cover last pin with centre 2 prs and WS TW.
8. Use left 2 prs to make a plt to next block diagonally left, and right 2 prs to make a plt to block diagonally right, allowing the single prs from square tallies to work in WS through each plt at the half-way point.

In dieser Variante wird der LS-Block anstatt mit 6 nur mit 3 N. wie folgt ausgeführt (siehe Zeichnung):
1. Bei *A* 2 P. einhäkeln, FL bis zum 1. N.-Punkt des Blocks klöppeln.
2. 2 P. bei *B* einhäkeln, FL bis zum 1. N.-Punkt des Blocks klöppeln.
3. Mit den 2 mittleren P. einen GZS ausführen, N. in die Mitte stechen.
4. GZS mit den 2 linken P., keine N.
5. GZS mit den 2 rechten P., keine N.
6. Punkte (3, 4 und 5) 2x wdh.

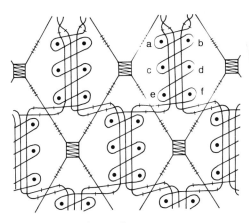

Toad in the Hole

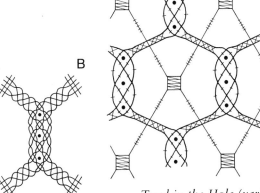

Toad in the Hole (variation 1)

7. Letzte N. mit GZS mit den 2 mittleren P. schließen.

8. Mit den 2 linken P. schräg nach links einen FL bis zum nächsten Block, dann mit den 2 rechten P. schräg nach rechts einen FL bis zum rechten Block ausführen, dabei durchläuft das Formschlag-Einzelpaar diesen FL in der Mitte im LS.

In deze variatie is het lsl blok over zes spelden, vervangen door drie spelden, die als volgt worden gewerkt (*zie* detail diagram):

1. Hang 2 pr in bij *A*, vl naar eerste speld van het blok.
2. Hang 2 pr in bij *B*, vl naar eerste speld van het blok.
3. Met 2 middelste prn lsl dr, speld ertussen.
4. Met 2 linkerprn, lsl dr, geen speld.
5. Met 2 rechterprn lsl dr, geen speld.
6. Herhaal (3, 4, en 5) 2x.
7. Sluit laatste speld met 2 midden prn, lsl dr.
8. Maak met 2 linkerprn een vl diagonaal naar het volgende blok links, en maak met 2 rechterprn een vl diagonaal naar volgende blok rechts, terwijl de enkele prn van de moezen in lsl door het midden van de vln gaan.

Pour cette variation, on remplace le pavé toilé de 6 épingles par 3 épingles travaillées comme suit:

1. Accrocher 2 p. sur *A* = C4 jusqu'à la première ép. du pavé.
   Accrocher 2 p. sur *B* = C4 jusqu'à la première ép. du pavé.

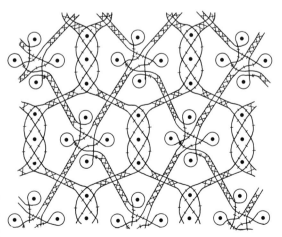

Toad in the Hole (variation 2)

3. Avec les 2p. du centre = pt dble, ép de soutien.
4. Avec les 2 p. à gauche = pt dble sans ép.
5. Avec les 2 p. à droite = pt dble sans ép.
6. Répéter (3, 4 et 5) × 2.
7. Fermer la dernière ép. avec les 2 p. centrales en pt dble.
8. Les 2 p. de gauche suivent la diagonale de gauche en C4 jusqu'au prochain pavé. Les ép. de droite suivent la diagonale de droite en C4 jusqu'au prochain pavé. Ces cordes sont respectivement coupées en leur milieu par les paires issues du point d'esprit carré. Rencontre en pt toile.

Toad in the Hole (variation 2)

1. To work each group of 3 pinholes use the same method as for 'Toad in the Hole (variation 1)'.
2. To work each group of 4 pinholes use the same method as for 'Blossom'.
3. Where plts cross each other, work a 4-plt crossing:
   (**i**) Cross centre 2 prs left over right
   (**ii**) TW left 2 prs right over left
   (**iii**) TW right 2 prs right over left
   (**iv**) Cross centre 2 prs left over right.

1. Jeder Block mit 3 N.-Punkten ist wie bei Variante *1* auszuführen.
2. Jede Gruppe mit 4 N.-Punkten wird wie beim 'Blossom'-Grund ausgeführt.
3. Die FL werden wie folgt gekreuzt:
   (i) die 2 mittleren P. links über rechts kr.
   (ii) die 2 linken P. rechts über links dr.
   (iii) die 2 rechten P. rechts über links dr.
   (iv) die 2 mittleren P. links über rechts kr.

1. Gebruik voor iedere groep van 3 spelden dezelfde methode als voor 'Toad in the Hole' (variatie 1).
2. Klos iedere groep van 4 spelden op dezelfde manier als 'Blossom'.
3. Klos, waar vln elkaar kruisen, een 4-vl kruising:
   (i) Kruis middelste 2 prn links over rechts
   (ii) Draai linker 2 prn rechts over links
   (iii) Draai rechter 2 prn rechts over links
   (iv) Kruis middelste 2 prn links over rechts

1. Chaque groupe de 3 ép. sera travaillé selon la méthode 'Toad in the Hole (variation 1)'.
2. Chaque groupe de 4 ép. suit la méthode décrite pour 'Blossom'.
3. Croisement des 2 C4 comme suit:
   (i) 2p centre = croiser p. gche sur p. dte
   (ii) 2p gauche = tourner p. dte sur p. gche
   (iii) 2p droite = tourner p. dte sur p. gche
   (iv) 2p centre = croiser p. gche sur p. dte

Four Pin

1. Sew in 2 prs above each pin.
2. Work WS with each group of 2 prs, pin between them, TW each pr 3 times.
3. With centre 2 prs work WS, TW both 3 times (no pin).
4. With left 2 prs work WS, TW both 3 times (no pin).
5. With right 2 prs work WS, TW both 3 times (no pin).
6. Repeat 3.
7. Place a pin between left 2 prs and another pin between right 2 prs.
8. Repeat 2–7 for each group of 4 prs.

1. Über jeden N.-Punkt 2 P. einhäkeln.
2. GZS mit jeder Gruppe von 2 P., Nadel dazwischen stecken, 2x dr.
3. GZS mit den 2 mittleren P., 2x dr. (keine N.)
4. GZS mit den 2 linken P., 2x dr. (keine N.)
5. GZS mit den 2 rechten P., 2x dr. (keine N.)

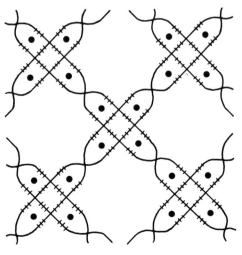

Four Pin

6. Punkt *3* wdh.
7. Je eine N. zwischen die 2 linken P. und die 2 rechten P. stecken.
8. Für jede Gruppe von 4 P. Punkt *2–7* wdh.

1. Hang boven iedere speld 2 pr in.
2. Klos met iedere groep van 2 pr lsl, speld ertussen, dr ieder pr 3 keer.
3. Met 2 middenprn lsl, dr beide 3 keer (geen speld).
4. Met 2 linker prn lsl, dr beide 3 keer (geen speld).
5. Met 2 rechter prn lsl, dr beide 3 keer (geen speld).
6. Herhaal **3**.
7. Zet een speld tussen 2 linker prn en een andere speld tussen 2 rechter prn.
8. Herhaal **2–7** voor iedere groep van 4 pr.

1. Accrocher 2 p. au-dessus de chaque pt d'ép.
2. Pt t., ép. pour chaque groupe, 3 t. chaque p.
3. Avec les 2 p. centre = pt t. sans ép., 3 t., chaque p.
4. 2 p. gche = pt t. sans ép., 3 t. chaque p.
5. 2 p. dte = pt t. sans ép., 3 t. chaque p.
6. Répéter **3**.
7. Mettre une èp. entre les 2 p. à gche, une èp. entre les 2 p. à dte.
8. Répéter **2** à **7** pour chaque groupe de 4 ép.

Jubilee

1. Each group of 4 prs is worked as for 'Four Pin', as far as **7**.
2. After **7**, the pin is covered with WS, TW both 3 times.
3. Each group of 2 prs travels diagonally so that 2 prs from left and 2 prs from right work the following:
   (i) With centre 2 prs work WS (no pin)
   (ii) With left 2 prs work WS (no pin
   (iii) With right 2 prs work WS (no pin)
   (iv) Repeat (i).
4. TW all prs 3 times.
5. Repeat from **2** of 'Four Pin'.

1. Mit jeder Gruppe von 4 P. wird wie beim 'Four Pin'-Grund bis Punkt *7* verfahren.
2. Nach *7* die N. mit GZS und 2x dr. schließen.
3. Jede 2-P.-Gruppe läuft diagonal, d.h. mit je 2 P. von links und rechts wie folgt arbeiten:
   (i) LS mit den 2 mittleren P. (keine N.)
   (ii) LS mit den 2 linken P. (keine N.)
   (iii) LS mit den 2 rechten P. (keine N.)
   (iv) Ab *I* wdh.
4. Alle P. 3x dr.
5. Ab Punkt **2** des 'Four Pin'-Grundes wdh.

1. Iedere groep van 4 pr wordt geklost als 'Four Pin', tot aan **7**.
2. Na **7**, wordt de speld gesloten met lsl, beide 3x dr.
3. Iedere groep van 2 pr loopt diagonaal verder, zodat 2 pr van links en 2 pr van rechs het volgende doen:
   (i) Met 2 middenprn lsl (geen speld)
   (ii) Met 2 linkerprn lsl (geen speld)
   (iii) Met 2 rechterprn lsl (geen speld)
   (iv) Herhaal (**i**).
4. Dr alle prn 3 keer.
5. Herhaal vanaf **2** uit 'Four Pin'.

1. Chaque groupe de 4 p. suit la méthode 'Four Pin' jusqu'à **7**.
2. Après **7**, fermer l'ép. en pt t. et 3 t. sur chaque p.
3. Chaque groupe de 2 p. suit une diagonale et se coupe comme suit:
   (i) 2 p. centre = pt t. sans ép.
   (ii) 2 p. gche = pt t. sans ép.
   (iii) 2 p. dte = pt t. sans ép.
   (iv) reprendre à (**i**).
4. 3 t. sur chaque p.
5. Reprendre à **2** méthode 'Four Pin'.

Italian

1. Sew in 2 prs at *A*, *B*, *C*, and *D*, and work WS with each group of 2 prs.
2. TW each pr 3 times, work diagonal prs in WS (no pin), then TW each pr 3 times.
3. Work diagonal prs in WS (no pin).
4. Sew in 1 pr at *E*, use as runners to work to left, * work 2 WS, TW

Jubilee

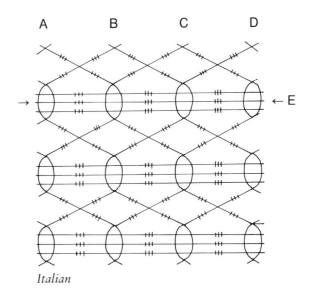

Italian

runners 3 times **. Repeat from *
to ** to the end and sew in.

5. Use same pr of runners to return to the right, * work 2 WS, TW runners 3 times **. Repeat from * to ** to the end and sew in.
6. Using the same pr of runners, return to the left as in 4 from *.
7. Work WS with each group of 2 prs passives before continuing from 2.

1. Je 2 P. bei A, B, C und D einhäkeln und GZS mit jeder 2-P.-Gruppe ausführen.
2. Jedes P. 2x dr., GZS mit den diagonal verlaufenden P. (ohne N.), jedes P. 2x dr.
3. LS mit den diagonal verlaufenden P. (keine N.)
4. Bei E 1 P. einhäkeln, als Laufp. nach links führen, *2x LS, Laufp. 3x dr. **. Von * bis ** bis zum Ende wdh. und abhäkeln.
5. Mit demselben Laufp. nach rechts zurückklöppeln, *2x LS, Laufp. 3x dr. **. Von * bis ** bis zum Ende wdh. und abhäkeln.
6. Mit demselben Laufp. nach links wie bei 4 ab* zurückkehren.
7. Mit jeder Gruppe von 2 Rißp. einen LS klöppeln, dann ab Punkt 2 wdh.

1. Hang 2 pr in bij A, B, C, en D, en klos lsl met iedere groep van 2 pr.
2. Dr elk pr 3 keer, klos met diagonale prn lsl (geen speld), dr dan ieder pr 3 keer.

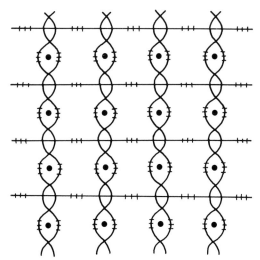

Pin and a Chain

3. Klos lsl met diagonale prn (geen speld).
4. Hang bij E 1 pr in, gebruik dat als looppaar naar links, * 2x lsl, dr looppaar 3 keer **. Herhaal van * tot ** tot aan het eind van de rij en haak aan.
5. Gebruik hetzelfde looppaar om naar rechts terug te keren, * 2x lsl, dr looppaar 3 keer **, Herhaal van * tot ** tot aan het eind en haak aan.
6. Keer met dezelfde lopers terug naar links zoals in 4 vanaf*.
7. Klos lsl met iedere groep van 2 hangende prn alvorens door te gaan vanaf 2.

1. Accrocher 2 p. sur A, B, C et D = pt t. avec chaque groupe de 2 p.
2. 3 t. sur chaque p. Travailler en diagonale en pt t. sans ép. puis 3 t. chaque p.
3. Rencontre des diagonales en pt t. sans ép.
4. Accrocher 1 p. sur E. L'utiliser comme voyageur vers la gche et faire * 2p. pt t., 3 t. des voyageurs. ** Reprendre de * à ** jusqu'à l'extrémité et accrocher.
5. Avec la même p. de voyageurs revenir à dte * 2 p. pt t., 3 t. des voyageurs. ** Répéter de * à ** jusqu'au bout. Accrocher.
6. Avec la même p. de voyageurs, retourner à gauche et reprendre comme 4*.
7. Faire pt t. sur chaque groupe de passives toilées. Reprendre à 2.

Pin and a Chain

1. Sew in 2 prs above each pinhole, and work a WS with each group of 2 prs.
2. Sew in 1 pr of runners above and to the right of first pin, TW 3 times.
3. * Work WS through 2 prs to the left (no pin), TW runners 3 times **. Repeat from * to ** across all the prs to the left and sew in runners.
4. For each group of 2 prs work WS, TW both prs 3 times, pin between them and cover with WS.
5. Repeat 2, 3, and 4 until filling is complete.

1. Über jeder N. 2 P. einhäkeln, und mit jeder 2-P.-Gruppe im LS klöppeln.
2. Rechts oberhalb des 1. N.-Punktes 1 Laufp. einhäkeln, 3x dr.
3. *Im LS 2 P. nach links durchlaufen (keine N.), Laufp. 3x dr. **. Von * bis ** durch alle linken P. klöppeln und Laufp. abhäkeln.
4. Mit jeder 2-P.-Gruppe LS klöppeln, beide P. 3x dr., N. dazwischen stecken und mit LS schließen.
5. Punke 2, 3 und 4 wdh., bis die Füllung vollständig ist.

1. Hang boven iedere speld 2 pr in, en klos lsl met elke groep van 2 pr.
2. Hang 1 pr lopers boven en rechts van de eerste speld, dr 3 keer.
3. * Klos lsl door 2 pr naar links (geen speld), dr lopers 3 keer. ** Herhaal van * tot ** door alle prn naar links en haak lopers aan.
4. Klos met iedere groep van 2 pr lsl, dr beide prn 3 keer, speld ertussen en sluit met lsl.
5. Herhaal 2 3, en 4 tot de vulling klaar is.

1. Accrocher 2 p. au-dessus de chaque trou d'ép. pt t. avec chaque groupe de 2 p.
2. Accrocher 1 p. de voyageurs au-dessus et à dte de la première ép. 3 t.
3. * pt t. sans ép. sur 2 p. vers la gauche, 3t. des voyageurs. ** répéter de * à ** sur toute la largeur et accrocher les voyageurs à gauche.
4. Chaque groupe toilé se ferme en pt t., 3 t. sur chaque paire, ép., fermer l'ép. en pt t.
5. Répéter 2, 3 et 4 aussi souvent que nécessaire.

Pin and a Stitch

1. Each pin is worked with 2 prs.
2. TW each pr 3 times.
3. Work WS, TW both prs 3 times; pin between the prs.
4. Cover pin with WS, and TW both prs 3 times.

1. Jede N. wird mit 2 P. umklöppelt.
2. Jedes P. 3x dr.
3. LS, beide P. 3x dr., N. zwischen die P. stecken.

4. N. mit LS schließen, und beide P. 3x drehen.

1. Iedere speld wordt met 2 pr gewerkt.
2. Dr elk pr 3 keer.
3. Lsl, dr beide prn 3 keer, speld ertussen.
4. Sluit speld met lsl, en dr beide prn 3 keer.

1. Chaque ép. se travaille avec 2 p.
2. 3 t. sur chaque p.
3. Pt dble, ép. de soutien et 3 t. sur chaque p.
4. Fermer ép. en pt t. et 3 t. sur chaque p.

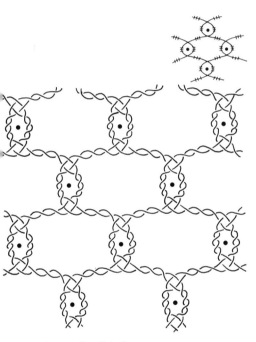

Pin and a Stitch

Trolly Net

1. Sew in 1 pr above each pinhole, and 1 pr runners to the right of first pin, TW each pr 4 times.
2. Take runners and work HS with next pr to left, pin between, TW both prs 4 times.
3. Repeat **2** across all the prs to the left and sew in runners.
4. Continue, following the diagram, by sewing in a new pr of runners to the right of next row of pinholes, and working **2** and **3**.

1. 1 P. über jedem N.-Punkt und ein Laufp. recht des ersten N.-Punktes einhäkeln; jedes P. 4x dr.
2. Mit Laufp. im Halbschlag nach links klöppeln, N. dazwischen stecken, beide P. 4x dr.
3. Punkt 2 wdh., indem man durch alle linken P. klöppelt, und Laufp. abhäkeln.
4. Nach Zeichnung fortfahren, wobei ein neues Laufp. rechts von der folgenden Reihe eingehäkelt wird, und Punkt 2–3 wdh.

1. Hang boven elke speld 1 pr in, en bovendien 1 looppaar rechts van de eerste speld, dr elk pr 4 keer.
2. Met lopers en volgende paar links nsl, speld ertussen, dr beide prn 4 keer.
3. Herhaal **2** met alle prn naar links en haak lopers aan.
4. Ga verder, volgens diagram, door rechts van de volgende rij spelden een nieuw pr in te hangen, en **2** en **3** te klossen.

1. Accrocher 1 p. au-dessus de chaque trou d'ép. et 1 p. de voyageurs à dte de la première ép., 4 t. sur chaque p.
2. Avec les voyageurs et la première p. sur la gche = pt s. et 4 t. sur chaque p., ép. de soutien.
3. Répéter **2** tout au long de la ligne et accrocher les voyageurs à gche.
4. Continuer selon le diagramme en accrochant une nouvelle p. de voyageurs à dte de chaque nouvelle rangée d'ép. Répéter **2** et **3**.

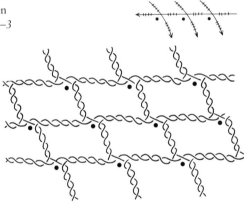

Trolly Net

Further Reading

DEVONIA, *The Honiton Lace Book* (The Bazaar Office, London, first published 1873; reprinted by Paul Minet, London, 1972)

LUXTON, ELSIE, *The Technique of Honiton Lace* (B.T. Batsford Ltd, first published 1979)

LUXTON, ELSIE, *Honiton Lace Patterns* (B.T. Batsford Ltd, first published 1983)

LUXTON, ELSIE and FUKUYAMA, YUSAI, *Honiton Lace: The Visual Approach* (B.T. Batsford, first published 1988)

LUXTON, ELSIE and FUKUYAMA, YUSAI, *Royal Honiton Lace* (B.T. Batsford, first published 1988)

LUXTON, ELSIE and FUKUYAMA, YUSAI, *Flowers in Honiton Lace* (B.T. Batsford, first published 1992)

MAIDMENT, MARGARET, *A Manual of Hand-Made Bobbin Lace* (Batsford 1931; reprinted by Piccadilly Rare Books, Paul Minet, London, 1983)

PALLISER, *The History of Lace* (E. P. Publishing Ltd, first published 1902)

PENDERAL MOODY A., *Devon Pillow Lace* (Cassell & Co Ltd, first published 1907)

TREADWIN, *Antique Point and Honiton Lace* (Ward Lock & Tyler, London, first published 1874)

Book Suppliers

AVON
Bridge Bookshop
7 Bridge Street
Bath BA2 4AS

Waterstone & Co.
4–5 Milsom Street
Bath BA1 1DA

BEDFORDSHIRE
Arthur Sells
Lane Cover
49 Pedley Lane
Clifton
Shefford SG17 5QT

BERKSHIRE
Loricraft
4 Big Lane
Lambourn

West End Lace Supplies
Ravensworth Court Road
Mortimer West End
Reading RG7 3UD

BUCKINGHAMSHIRE
J. S. Sear
Lacecraft Supplies
8 Hillview
Sherington MK16 9NJ

CAMBRIDGESHIRE
Dillons the Bookstore
Sidney Street
Cambridge

CHESHIRE
Lynn Turner
Church Meadow Crafts
7 Woodford Road
Winsford

CORNWALL
Creative Books
22A River Street
Truro TR1 2SJ

DEVON
Creative Crafts & Needlework
18 High Street
Totnes TQ9 5NP

Honiton Lace Shop
44 High Street
Honiton EX14 8PJ

DORSET
F. Herring & Sons
27 High West Street
Dorchester DT1 1UP

Tim Parker (*mail order*)
124 Corhampton Road
Boscombe East
Bournemouth BH6 5NZ

Christopher Williams
19 Morrison Avenue
Parkstone
Poole BH17 4AD

DURHAM
Lacemaid
6, 10 & 15 Stoneybeck
Bishop Middleham DL17 9BL

GLOUCESTERSHIRE
Southgate Handicrafts
63 Southgate Street
Gloucester GL1 1TX

Waterstone & Company
89–90 The Promenade
Cheltenham GL50 1NB

HAMPSHIRE
Creative Crafts
11 The Square
Winchester SO23 9ES

Doreen Gill
14 Barnfield Road
Petersfield GU31 4DR

Larkfield Crafts
4 Island Cottages
Mapledurwell
Basingstoke RG23 2LU

Needlestyle
24–26 West Street
Alresford

Ruskins
27 Bell Street
Romsey

ISLE OF WIGHT
Busy Bobbins
Unit 7
Scarrots Lane
Newport PO30 1JD

KENT
The Handicraft Shop
47 Northgate
Canterbury CT1 1BE

Hatchards
The Great Hall
Mount Pleasant Road
Tunbridge Wells

LONDON
W. & G. Foyle Ltd
113–119 Charing Cross Road
WC2H 0EB

Hatchards
187 Piccadilly W1V 9DA

MIDDLESEX
Redburn Crafts
Squires Garden Centre
Halliford Road
Upper Halliford
Shepperton TW17 8RU

NORFOLK
Alby Lace Museum
Cromer Road
Alby
Norwich NR11 7QE

Jane's Pincushions
Taverham Craft Unit 4
Taverham Nursery Centre
Fir Covert Road
Taverham
Norwich NR8 6HT

Waterstone & Company Ltd
30 London Street
Norwich NR2 1LD

NORTHAMPTONSHIRE
Denis Hornsby
149 High Street
Burton Latimer
Kettering NN15 5RL

SOMERSET
Bridge Bookshop
62 Bridge Street
Taunton TA1 1UD

STAFFORDSHIRE
J. & J. Ford (*mail order & lace days only*)
October Hill
Upper Way
Upper Longdon
Rugeley WS15 1QB

SUSSEX
Waterstone & Company Ltd
120 Terminus Road
Eastbourne

WARWICKSHIRE
Christine & David Springett
21 Hillmorton Road
Rugby CV22 6DF

WILTSHIRE
Everyman Bookshop
5 Bridge Street
Salisbury SP1 2ND

NORTH YORKSHIRE
Craft Basics
9 Gillygate
York

Shireburn Lace
Finkle Court
Finkle Hill
Sherburn in Elmet LS25 6EB

The Craft House
23 Bar Street
Scarborough YO13 9QE

WEST MIDLANDS
Needlewoman
21 Needles Alley
off New Street
Birmingham B2 5AG

WEST YORKSHIRE
Sebalace
Waterloo Mill
Howden Road
Silsden BD20 0HA

George White Lacemaking Supplies
40 Heath Drive
Boston Spa LS23 6PB

Just Lace
Lacemaker Supplies
14 Ashwood Gardens
Gildersome
Leeds LS27 7AS

Jo Firth
58 Kent Crescent
Lowtown, Pudsey
Leeds LS28 9EB

SCOTLAND
Embroidery Shop
51 William Street
Edinburgh
Lothian EH3 7LW

Waterstone & Company Ltd
236 Union Street
Aberdeen AB1 1TN

WALES
Bryncraft Bobbins (*mail order*)
B. J. Phillips
Pantglas
Cellan
Lampeter
Dyfed SA48 8JD

Hilkar Lace Suppliers
33 Mysydd Road
Landore
Swansea

Equipment Suppliers

UNITED KINGDOM

BEDFORDSHIRE
A. Sells
49 Pedley Lane
Clifton
Shefford SG17 5QT

BERKSHIRE
Chrisken Bobbins
26 Cedar Drive
Kingsclere RG15 8TD

Loricraft (*general and bobbins*)
4 Big Lane
Lambourn

West End Lace Supplies (*general and bobbins*)
Ravensworth Court Road
Mortimer West End
Reading RG7 3UD

BUCKINGHAMSHIRE
Bartlett, Caesar and Partners
(*bobbins and lace pillows*)
12 Creslow Court
Stony Stratford
Milton Keynes MK11 1NN

J. S. Sear
Lacecraft Supplies
8 Hillview
Sherington MK16 9NJ

Sizelands
1 Highfield Road
Winslow MK10 3QU

SMP
4 Garners Close
Chalfont St Peter SL9 0HB

CAMBRIDGESHIRE
Heffers Graphic Shop (*matt coloured transparent adhesive film*)
26 King Street
Cambridge CB1 1LN

Ken & Pat Schultz
134 Wisbech Road
Thornley
Peterborough

Spangles
Carole Morris
Cashburn Lane
Burwell CB5 0ED

CHESHIRE
Lynn Turner
Church Meadow Crafts
7 Woodford Road
Winsford

DEVON
Honiton Lace Shop
44 High Street
Honiton EX14 8PJ

DORSET
Frank Herring & Sons
27 High West Street
Dorchester DT1 1UP

T. Parker (*mail order, general and bobbins*)
124 Corhampton Road
Boscombe East
Bournemouth BH6 5NZ

ESSEX
Needlework
Ann Bartleet
Bucklers Farm
Coggeshall CO6 1SB

GLOUCESTERSHIRE
T. Brown (*bobbins*)
Temple Lane Cottage
Littledean
Cinderford

Chosen Crafts Centre
46 Winchcombe Street
Cheltenham GL52 2ND

HAMPSHIRE
Bartlett, Caesar and Partners
(*bobbins and lace pillows*)
The Glen
Shorefield Road
Downton
Lymington SO41 0LH

Busy Bobbins
Unit 7
Scarrots Lane
Newport
IOW PO30 1JD

Larkfield Crafts (*bobbins*)
Hilary Ricketts
4 Island Cottages
Mapledurwell
Basingstoke RG23 2LU

Needlestyle
24–26 West Street
Alresford

Newnham Lace Equipment (*lace pillows*)
15 Marlowe Close
Basingstoke RG24 9DD

KENT
The Handicraft Shop
47 Northgate
Canterbury CT1 1BE

Denis Hornsby
25 Manwood Avenue
Canterbury CT2 7AH

Frances Iles
73 High Street
Rochester ME1 1LX

LANCASHIRE
Malcolm J. Fielding (*bobbins*)
2 Northern Terrace
Moss Lane
Silverdale LA5 0ST

MERSEYSIDE
Hayes & Finch
Head Office & Factory
Hanson Road
Aintree
Liverpool L9 9BP

MIDDLESEX
Redburn Crafts
Squires Garden Centre
Halliford Road
Upper Halliford
Shepperton TW17 8RU

NORFOLK
Alby Lace Museum
Cromer Road
Alby
Norwich NR11 7QE

Jane's Pincushions
Taverham Craft Unit 4
Taverham Nursery Centre
Fir Covert Road
Taverham
Norwich NR8 6HT

Jane Playford
North Lodge
Church Close
West Runton NR27 9QY

Richard Viney (*bobbins*)
Unit 7
Port Royal Street
Southsea PO5 3UD

George Walker
The Corner Shop
Rickinghall, Diss

NORTH HUMBERSIDE
Teazle Embroideries
35 Boothferry Road
Hull

NORTH YORKSHIRE
The Craft House
23 Bar Street
Scarborough

Shireburn Lace
Finkle Court
Finkle Hill
Sherburn in Elmet LS25 6EB

Stitchery
Finkle Street
Richmond

NORTHANTS
Denis Hornsby
149 High Street
Burton Latimer
Kettering NN15 5RL

SOUTH YORKSHIRE
D. H. Shaw
47 Lamor Crescent
Thrushcroft
Rotherham S66 9QD

STAFFORDSHIRE
J. & J. Ford (*mail order and lace days only*)
October Hill
Upper Way
Upper Longdon
Rugeley WS15 1QB

SUFFOLK
A. R. Archer (*bobbins*)
The Poplars
Shetland
near Stowmarket IP14 3DE

Mary Collins (*linen by the metre, and made up articles of church linen*)
Church Furnishings
St Andrews Hall
Humber Doucy Lane
Ipswich IP4 3BP

E. & J. Piper (*silk embroidery and lace thread*)
Silverlea
Flax Lane
Glemsford CO10 7RS

SURREY
Needle and Thread
80 High Street
Horsell
Woking GU21 4SZ

Needlestyle
5 The Woolmead
Farnham GU9 7TX

SUSSEX
Southern Handicrafts
20 Kensington Gardens
Brighton BN1 4AC

WARWICKSHIRE
Christine & David Springett
21 Hillmorton Road
Rugby CV22 5DF

WEST MIDLANDS
Framecraft
83 Hampstead Road
Handsworth Wood
Birmingham B2 1JA

Framecraft Miniatures Ltd (frames
   and mounts)
148–150 High Street
Aston
Birmingham B6 4US

The Needlewoman
21 Needles Alley
off New Street
Birmingham B2 5AE

Stitches
Dovehouse Shopping Parade
Warwick Road
Olton, Solihull

WEST YORKSHIRE
Jo Firth
Lace Marketing & Needlecraft
   Supplies
58 Kent Crescent
Lowtown
Pudsey LS28 9EB

Just Lace
Lacemaker Supplies
14 Ashwood Gardens
Gildersome
Leeds LS27 7AS

Sebalace
Waterloo Mills
Howden Road
Silsden BD20 0HA

George White Lacemaking Supplies
40 Heath Drive
Boston Spa LS23 6PB

WILTSHIRE
Doreen Campbell (frames and
   mounts)
Highcliff
Bremilham Road
Malmesbury SN16 0DQ

WORCESTERSHIRE
Richard Gravestock (general and
   bobbins)
Highwood
Crews Hill
Alfrick WR6 5HF

SCOTLAND
Christine Riley
53 Barclay Street
Stonehaven
Kincardineshire

Peter & Beverley Scarlett
Strupak
Hill Head
Cold Wells, Ellon
Grampian

WALES
Bryncraft Bobbins
B. J. Phillips
Pantglas
Cellan
Lampeter
Dyfed SA48 8JD

Hilkar Lace Suppliers
33 Mysydd Road
Landore
Swansea

AUSTRALIA
Australian Lace magazine
P.O. Box 1291
Toowong
Queensland 4066

Dentelles Lace Supplies
c/o Betty Franks
39 Lang Terrace
Northgate 4013
Brisbane
Queensland

The Lacemaker
94 Fordham Avenue
Hartwell
Victoria 3124

Spindle and Loom
Arcade 83
Longueville Road
Lane Cove
NSW 2066

Tulis Crafts
201 Avoca Street
Randwick
NSW 2031

BELGIUM
't Handwerkhuisje
Katelijnestraat 23
8000 Bruges

Kantcentrum
Balstraat 14
8000 Bruges

Manufacture Belge de Dentelle
6 Galerie de la Reine
Galeries Royales St Hubert
1000 Bruxelles

Orchidée
Mariastraat 18
8000 Bruges

Ann Thys
't Apostelientje
Balstraat 11
8000 Bruges

FRANCE
Centre d'Initiations à la Dentelle
   du Puy
2 Rue Duguesclin
43000 Le Puy en Vela

A L'Econome
Anne-Marie Deydier
Ecole de Dentelle aux Fuseaux
10 rue Paul Chenavard
69001 Lyon

Rougier and Plé
13–15 Bd des Filles de Calvaire
75003 Paris

WEST GERMANY
Der Fenster Laden
Berliner Str. 8
D 6483 Bad Soden
Salmünster

P. P. Hempel
Ortolanweg 34
1000 Berlin

HOLLAND
Blokker's Boektiek
Bronsteeweg 4/4a
2101 AC Heemstede

Theo Brejaart
Dordtselaan 146–148
PO Box 5199
3008 AD Rotterdam

Heikina de Rüyter
Zuiderstraat 1
9693 ER Nieweschans

Magazijn De Vlijt
Lijnmarkt 48
Utrecht

SWITZERLAND
Fadehax
Inh. Irene Solca
4105 Biel-Benken
Basel

NEW ZEALAND
Peter McLeavey
P.O. Box 69.007
Auckland 8

USA
Arbor House
22 Arbor Lane
Roslyn Heights
NY 11577

Baltazor Inc.
3262 Severn Avenue
Metairie
LA 7002

Beggars' Lace
P.O. Box 17263
Denver
Colo 80217

Berga Ullman Inc.
P.O. Box 918
North Adams
MA 01247

Frederick J. Fawcett
129 South Street
Boston
MA 02130

Frivolité
15526 Densmore N.
Seattle
WA 98113

Happy Hands
3007 S. W. Marshall
Pendleton
Oreg 97180

International Old Lacers
P.O. Box 1029
Westminster
Colo 80030

Lace Place de Belgique
800 S. W. 17th Street
Boca Raton
FL 33432

Lacis
2150 Stuart Street
Berkeley
CA 9470

Robin's Bobbins
RTL Box 1736
Mineral Bluff
GA 30559

Robin and Russ
Handweavers
533 North Adams Street
McMinnvills
Oreg 97128

Some Place
2990 Adline Street
Berkeley
CA 94703

Osma G. Todd Studio
319 Mendoza Avenue
Coral Gables
FL 33134

The Unique And Art Lace Cleaners
5926 Delman Boulevard
St Louis
MO 63112

Van Scriver Bobbin Lace
130 Cascadilla Park
Ithaca
NY 14850

The World in Stitches
82 South Street
Milford
N.H. 0305

Sources of Information

UNITED KINGDOM

The British College of Lace
21 Hillmorton Road
Rugby
War CV22 5DF

The English Lace School
Oak House
Church Stile
Woodbury
Nr Exeter
Devon EX5 1HP

The Lace Guild
The Hollies
53 Audnam
Stourbridge
West Midlands DY8 4AE

The Lacemakers' Circle
49 Wardwick
Derby DE1 1HY

The Lace Society
Linwood
Stratford Road
Oversley
Alcester
War BY9 6PG

Ring of Tatters
Miss B. Netherwood
269 Oregon Way
Chaddesden
Derby DE2 6UR

United Kingdom Director of International Old Lacers
S. Hurst
4 Dollis Road
London N3 1RG

OIDFA
(International Bobbin and Needle Lace Organization)
Chair
Suzanne Puech
3 Chemin de Parenty
F-69250 Neuville sur Saône
France

BELGIUM

OIDFA/Belgische Kantorganisatie
Lydia Thiels-Mertens
Jagersberg 1
B-3294 Molenstede-Diest

FRANCE

OIDFA
Suzanne Puech
3 Chemin de Parenty
F-69250 Neuville sur Saône

GERMANY

OIDFA
Uta Ulrich
Papenbergweg 33
D-4930 Detmold

Deutscher Klöppelverband e.V.
Ortolanweg 7
D-100 Berlin 47

THE NETHERLANDS

OIDFA
Puck Smelter-Hoekstra
Corona 68
NL-3204 CM Spijkenisse

LOKK
Boterbloem 56
NL-7322 GX Apeldoorn

USA

OIDFA
Kathy Kauffmann
1301 Greenwood
Wilmette
Illinois 60091

International Old Lacers
Gunvor Jorgensen (Pres.)
366 Bradley Avenue
Northvale
NR 076647

Lace & Crafts magazine
3201 East Lakeshore Drive
Tallahassee
FL 32312-2034

Grid Prickings for Fillings

Whole Stitch Block

Toad in the Hole

Four Pin

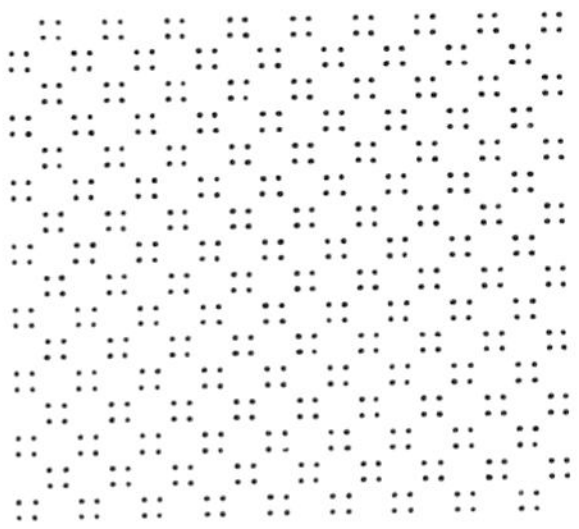

Pin and a Chain

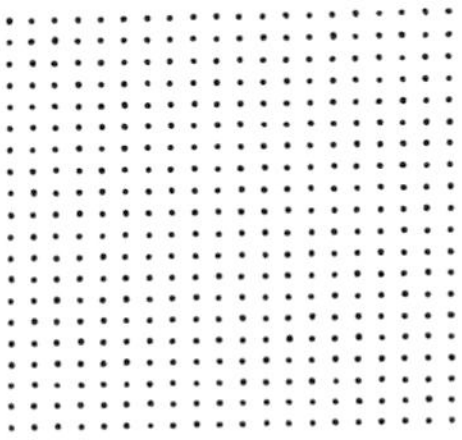

Whole Stitch Block Variation

Toad in the Hole (variation 1)

Jubilee

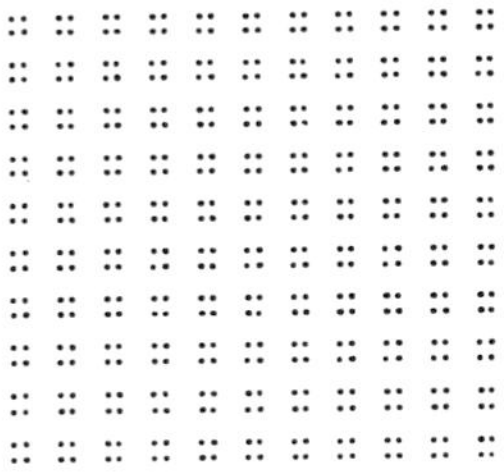

Pin and a Stitch

Trolley Net

Blossom

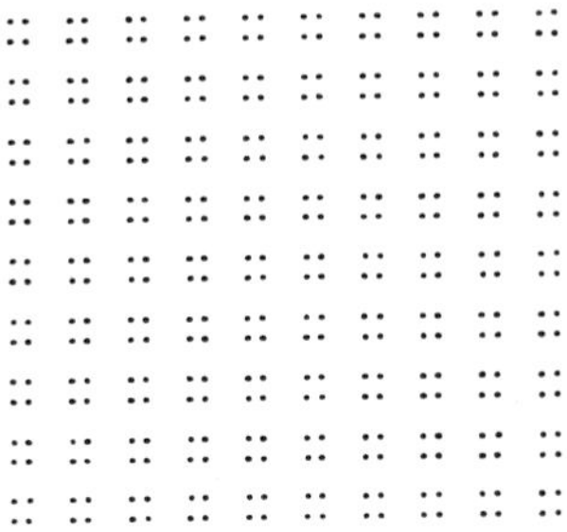